CONTENT WRITING AND MARKETING

How to Write Content That Converts and Become
a Successful Entertainer

(Build an Engaged Audience for Your Personal
Brand Through)

Angel Ortiz

Published By Angel Ortiz

Angel Ortiz

Content Writing and Marketing: How to Write Content That Converts and Become a Successful Entertainer (Build an Engaged Audience for Your Personal Brand Through)

ISBN 978-1-77485-429-7

Legal & Disclaimer

TABLE OF CONTENTS

Introduction

The word refers to the set of words that users can read while visiting websites via the Internet.

With the advent of the Internet Content writing is slowly becoming a profession that is well-known.

In contrast to Western countries where content writing is a second sources of revenue, India has seen tremendous growth in this field.

Many people from all different walks of life choose this field. Many believe that producing content is a straightforward job that anyone can master it, however in reality it requires a lot of determination, an interest in reading and a genuine production.

Components that are integrated when creating content

It's easy to write content however, it's actually an exhausting task.

He is a promising writer and a good pay. There are some things that are considered to be the most important aspects for content writers. The following are among them:

Writing content is dependent on doing research about a specific subject.

Only content writers who have the ability to meet the standards that research attaches high importance to and cleverly blend their personal perceptions with outcomes that are derived from research.

Content writing on any topic requires a lot of analytical thinking and innovative approaches. Content writers craft articles that are both web-friendly as well as readers-friendly.

Content writers must be able to comprehend the nuances of the business of his client.

Paying attention to the employer's efforts and incorporating them in the Bible is the work of the content writer.

3 Excellent language skills as well as the capacity to voice opinions are essential to writing content that every content writer needs to possess.

In recent times the writing of content has turned into writing that is used to market the product or service.

Content writers can encourage readers to buy their products through their writing.

They must be innovative so that their writing could influence the reader to purchase the product they are interested in.

The primary reason to write articles is making the site well-known to search engines. In order to do this, writers write content that is rich in keywords.

Similar to any other job it is a matter of determination, dedication as well as the desire to do your job to be an effective content writer.

These are just a few of the qualities of a good writer, which are covered in this class. Certain essential characteristics are highlighted many times.

If you have the qualities of a good writing content, but you are not going to succeed. You must practice them , and then enhance your writing abilities.

Then you can become an excellent writer in the blink of an eye.

Chapter 1: How To Become A Better Content Writer

Create the title and content of the essays.
Basics of Content Writing have published this book following thorough research.

This book is a small one on writing content. In this course , you'll discover a wealth of writing tips and lots of clever writing tricks that can aid you in improving your writing abilities.

This course can aid you in improving your writing abilities. It's the base of every marketing strategy. Before we begin this course, I'd like to introduce myself.

I am extremely interested in this subject , and I would love to learn more about the exciting possibilities this medium offers.

I've passed on this information via online courses and through my blog.

In addition, I've written several classes that are available on NY DAG and have enrolled more than 11,000 students into these courses.

Let's discuss the discussions topics. Everybody has writing abilities regardless of the industry they work in. Similar to other skills.

Writing is also a process that requires practice before getting to this point.

In the beginning, you should begin writing with this idea in your mind. Let me present to you an overview of the letter of Miss Lemark.

Her name is American author as well as a non-fiction writer and writing instructor. The body of nearly all great writing starts with terrible first drafts.

It is necessary to begin somewhere. The only way to master writing is to begin writing, and then write. Even after starting we often attempt to write early as we're novices to writing.

It's not because of our expectations or the other terrible efforts mentioned in the quote that we are prone to think we don't have the technology or ability to write. In reality, at the very least some practice could have helped us become better writers.

Better than what we were initially certified to accomplish. I am saying this to stress that anyone can be an author.

and he is able to create content when he has three things that are essential such as a basic understanding of the language, the ability to use a laptop or desktop computer connected to the internet and three hours of striving to create.

It is also the most crucial quality. It is widely acknowledged that content writing is an area that is related to online writing and content creators for web marketing campaigns can be used to give examples of content that has been returned for production websites that are dedicated to Products are being developed. Market or sell a company or brand. The content will bring people to these websites and convert them into their customers.

The contents of SEO campaign marketing can be found here. Content is generated by a combination of keywords or phrases that have been researched by marketers.

These are the most searched for words or phrases in relation to a specific subject.

The quality of content that is produced in these instances will be determined through the correct quantity of keywords that are introduced throughout this document.

Then, what are the two different cases of creating content? This indicates that creating content requires different skills , and the skills required are not necessarily identical.

Content writers must have the skills such as the capacity to write with ease on a variety of subjects and to produce the proper amount of keywords that are predetermined in an article without compromising the readability. Two of the most important skills that a content writer must be able to perform.

Each writer should try to improve these skills in order be better at writing. Continue. Let's look at the reasons to become a content creator.

What makes content writing an excellent choice? What are the advantages of becoming an author of content? The answers to these questions will provide you some reasons to become a content writer.

Before I get into the meat of the issue Let me show you an easy step. These are just a few ideas to help you make the decision to pursue a career in writing.

If you're obsessed with writing, but do not share that passion, it's more difficult to become a professional author.

This is an important issue in the present and we'll look deeper into the court.

The issue of writing enthusiasm is a subject that will be raised when we look at the ability of an individual to write.

When you have a chance to evaluate the quality of your writing ability it will be simpler for you to figure out whether you have the drive to continue.

Whatever the genuine love for writing has to be, it is essential to be a writer as a full-time business in Korea Content writing is among many of the highest-paying and exciting job opportunities in the field of today's marketing.

One of the main reasons for this growth is the rise in the use of digital marketing.

Digital marketing is a standard marketing technique used by the advertising industry of today.

The increasing market for digital marketing has increased need for marketing content, and consequently content writing.

Thus, the demand for content writers is always growing and many Fords are expected to increase.

We now realize that content writing is an a crucial aspect of marketing, I'll begin by highlighting some advantages of writing content in this particular context. I would suggest that writing content is an easy task.

If you look at the field it is common to find some degree of difficulty or trouble that is associated with a job.

We'd say it's a tough job and that the work demands a lot of preparation and there are many obstacles to overcome for this extras' business.

These aren't things that can affect your work, such as creating content as content writer. It is enough to know English well and be proficient in your grammar.

These two traits will help you become an effective content writer. as with any other occupation to be a successful writer, you must be able to influence your writing.

That's it. I'll give you an additional advantage by choosing a writing profession that allows you to be professional writers.

If you're just proficient in your native language and the main point is that it's not necessary to attend particular or meritorious schools to get started or to write an assignment or job. You will only be able to start your career once you're moving.

If you don't start writing, you'll have the possibility of writing about any subject. You are free to write content on a variety of subjects from travel to food to lifestyle and much more.

If you're interested involved in a particular niche and aren't aware about it, you could investigate and write about it.

It makes the work of a content creator easier and to many authors, the type of research can make their work more exciting and enjoyable.

This isn't something typical of many jobs we perform within the current industry.

Let me share with you the greatest benefit of selecting content writing as a career.

Writing content is an form of writing that allows professionals to be independent. A lot of writers in the field like this option.

There's no room for freedom in many of the other jobs available in the present market This is among the main reasons many people believe that content writing is a fantastic career option.

Additionally you can also pick your job, and even pick your field of interest and be able to work inside the walls that surround your house and make money from a something you love.

All you need is an internet connection to begin your service from there.

Begin your business by writing. You are paid according to the amount of articles you write and complete all that work at your home.

This makes content writing one of the most sought-after careers in the marketing industry.

Therefore, we have a solid reason to pick the field of content writing for our work.

Let me reiterate a second aspect that I believe is the best aspect of content writing. That is to consider this field with a deep enthusiasm for writing.

There is nothing more satisfying than working in a field that you love.

This is an advantage since we see that the majority of people complain that their job at Monotonies is dull.

If you've got an occupation that you are enthusiastic about then you'll be content and, in addition you'll never get bored.

Writing content is an additional chance that the majority of traditional professions do not. You can consider beginning a content writing company.

In the end, I'll describe in detail how to accomplish this and one option is to create an online site and write the content on your own.

You can also arrange other writers to write for you. Once you've created an account and added your contact information along with test papers, you can also add essential information, you can post it on the website.

If so, you've been in business since you first started hiring for content positions. Be sure to add this info to your site.

You can also include testimonials from your customers that will always be a good thing. So, you can build a successful publishing business.

Like I mentioned before that the tools are found in digital marketing. It propels the industry of content marketing to new standards.

If you're working in the field you will certainly appreciate the hard work you put into it. Content writing has become a necessity in the world of digital marketing today and digital marketing has become an everyday thing.

Contrary to the past where many businesses had the option of exempting it with little loss.

Every business nowadays requires an in-house team for content marketing or a project in content marketing and consequently an author.

This concludes this lecture in this lecture. It is clear that choosing to pursue content writing as a career has numerous advantages. We'll continue with different aspects of this course at on the following conference.

That's all. I'd like to thank you again for taking part in the course as well as for my efforts. Thank you for your time and I hope you have a wonderful day and continue to learn.

What editors compose

Have you been looking at the slogan on a newspaper advertisement and thought "I would have been able to write that!" Or "I could have come up with something better! "?

The good news isthat it's only getting better. Copywriting doesn't only pertain to newspapers - businesses also are able to meet a wide range of copy requirements!

Copying is defined as writing that is intended for business.

It's a type of marketing or selling - the aim is to draw customers to join your brand's community using whatever means you choose to use.

Each media (e.g. television, the internet, print packaging, etc.) is unique, with its own specifics, contexts, and challenges Your approach as a copywriter will differ.

Keep in mind that the needs are different for B2C (Business to Consumer) and B2B (Business to Business) because they both must be tailored to the mindset of the audience.

This is a non-exhaustive list of copy-writing requirements that companies might need to meet:

Advertising copy

Content Marketing

Advertising via email

Social media marketing

Marketing material (brochures, signs, etc.)

Manual

Product Name

Product Description

Press release

Social media posts

Home page

The product launches

Customer service script

Transactional emails

The sales team needs a script

Long sales letters

Web Information

Show

Radio advertising

Survey

Under the heading How to Be an Author, we'll look at how to become an excellent copywriter. We will also focus on the various types of business requirements.

If you have other forms of writing that you are interested in that we've not listed here Leave a comment below, and we'll add them as we grow our library here!

Chapter 2: Content Creator

We discovered that in nearly all instances, people sent the letter at the first try.

Quality of very first writing time is a disaster. We've learned that writing content can be linked to online writing We have also discovered that a skilled content writer can use the right amount of keywords into the text and ensure that the content doesn't disappear from its purpose. Readability. This conference

We also discussed the reasons one might be a content writer and we were able to answer a nagging query regarding that. We discussed the benefits of content writing as well as the advantages of operating.

Hope that the previous lecture or seminar provided you with the knowledge of an occupation in content writing. It is possible to pursue this writing for a part-time or as a full-time job. Let's begin an entirely new discussion and talk about the topic of our choice during this discussion.

A lot of successful content writers appear to enjoy a relaxed lifestyle. They can work from home, reduce their own inventory and can work as much or little as they'd like.

For all these reasons, a lot of us do not succeed in this particular area and this is due to the fact we are hesitant to write, as there are numerous reasons to not begin writing.

However, for a lot of us, it's the fear of being to the wrong place.

It's possible that you have a great concept, however it's not not a good idea. It's important to write it down on paper, and once the first draft, you'll know you're in a specific region.

And then you start to doubt. Just to let you know it seems you've left the right spot. I'm offering you another great quarter. This quarter fits in with the subject for this convention. So If you're hoping to become a writer create this corpus of Epictetus.

The code is extremely easy to understand. If we continue the discussion, you will be able to be able to understand the significance to this discussion. We'll try to figure out if you possess writing abilities or not.

This is vital and crucial if you're about to begin your writing career. This is since it won't be feasible for you to study Acadia in the absence of possess a knack for writing.

Although this field has many Elon instructors to choose from We know that writing is a simple job if you approach it in the right way and don't require a college qualification to be able to do it.

You'll need some fundamental skills to be a competent content writer. Now , the question is what can you do to determine whether you're a writer? The answer is in the work you do.

It's a good idea to begin writing and becoming an author. It is essential to begin writing. Then you can determine whether your writing ability is already there.

The first thing you need to do to find out whether you are gifted for writing is to begin writing. You are able to write on any topic.

Choose a subject you are interested in to write about, and then you've got your opinions on the subject. It is the only method to write you best writing is by considering subjects that you are familiar with and speak about.

If , after you've written your scripts on these topics , you have an enticing idea of your content, you might discover that you feel as if you're writing and are becoming a professional writer. It's important to practice and continue to practice and it is no sugar in this stage.

Let's examine this writing talent in greater in depth. It's a difficult problem to pinpoint.

Let me clarify that the reason behind this situation is mostly because the content is subjective matter.

The content can't be conclusively assessed and consequently the quality of writing cannot be evaluated right away.

A person's ability to write may be assessed and interpreted differently depending on the situation.

One of the criteria for judging writing talent is the quality of the content is to the reader. If an article is popular and communicates the main issues well, then the content is excellent.

Alongside content that readers love creative thinking is another aspect that is what makes content great.

I'll stay here for a while. I'll probably scare you by explaining all these features in the text and make it seem like writing is difficult work.

Don't let that deter you from describing all the traits of great content. Let's be honest that writing isn't an ability you acquire in the first day of your education.

Writing well is a skill that you acquire and learn as you go along. As I said at the beginning of this presentation the best method to evaluate your writing ability is to begin writing.

Once you have started writing, you must proceed. As you go you will improve your abilities and elevate your writing skills up a notch.

Through the process You can also get feedback from your readers and get an initial report about how well your work is written and then further improve it by fixing errors.

If you've completed something, I'll be truthful with you. Writing is a seemingly easy task, however becoming a proficient writer is a challenging work that is essential to you to be successful in your work.

It requires lots of practice. Be involved in lots of research. If you can do this consistently and consistently you'll become an effective and safe content writer.

I'd like to know a talent that doesn't require a lot of work. That's it. I'll end this discussion here in this discussion. We discussed ways to know whether we were able to create or not.

I want to express my gratitude again for the opportunity to re-engage me in my conversations as well as for supporting my efforts in education. We wish you wonderful day and to continue learning.

Chapter 3: The Qualities Of A Good Content Writer

There are many skills writers need to excel in this particular field.

If you'd like find out if you're making use of it, this article will help you improve the skills you need to succeed in this field.

You don't have to have all of the properties on this list and I'm sure there are many more I didn't include in this list.

What I'm trying to stress is that the best content authors in the world today did not have the features mentioned when they began their careers.

Don't worry in the event that you don't own one of the properties listed.

If you are inclined to write, you'll be able to build a large number of these skills independently.

Once you've purchased these products, they'll aid in improving your writing skills. Let's begin by listing the traits of a successful content writer.

One of the most fundamental ideas is a good understanding of the written language.

This is a fundamental requirement and successful writers are knowledgeable of the language they're playing with and are adept at grammar.

It's also a fundamental necessity. These virtues improve how well prose is written they write and is a reliable indication of a good content.

Even readers who are not familiar with grammar or language can appreciate the quality of information when they read it.

I'll tell you why, our world is a time that is characterized by people who have small attention spans and are constantly bombarded by the abundance of books to pick from.

This is a situation that requires high quality and quality content. These are the essential elements to draw readers.

I'd say Arby is a fan of good content and this is a must-have feature for any kind of content. Try it with papaya.

I spoke about this topic briefly in one of my previous lectures. I'll repeat this topic, and it's an intriguing title that should be an investigation worth doing.

You should have excellent research abilities. A thorough research process is crucial to any subject you write.

Writers who are good in this area have the unique ability of separating the key elements of a topic from their reading materials and then apply them to the content they've written.

It can help readers greatly as they're not subject to the hassle of every subject.

This is crucial for us today, since these days, there is many books about a particular topic via the internet.

It is not necessary to read through this entire details to find out more about a specific subject or to become an expert.

Sometimes, he can't gain the most wisdom from this materials. A skilled writer will have a chance to shine to shine here. It is possible to write articles that contain high-quality information.

They are like me because they are knowledgeable readers. They are quick to read and can search thousands of words, and then choose the most relevant information to incorporate in their writing. Sorting through a huge amount of information in a short time for best outcomes is a good-quality content. Content writers are a great important part of any project involving content marketing.

One of the advantages of our writers is the ability to write an article from scratch by conducting research on every new topic they will write about.

Good writers are able to develop new content based on research and present accurate information and information relevant to customers, and their knowledge is that they require lesser effort and less time to achieve this.

You can see the importance of this quality to have a good content.

What I'm going say here is the importance of quality, which will improve the quality of content writer's writing.

Do you have a lot of interest and desire for more information about the subject?

A great writer is naturally curious to know more. This is a characteristic that allows copywriters become more creative when writing content. It also consequently, assures that the content is unique and relevant. It also serves the goal to which it was created.

Here's another quality that every content writer should possess. It's a great proofreading. A great author is often a skilled proofreader.

The ability to see possible arrows within an article while writing helps writers come up with more effective and superior content.

This is a crucial role since many companies in the current marketplace cannot afford to employ an editor and copywriter at the same time. editor simultaneously.

Therefore, find writers who are able to perform a good job or have a high level of content.

Editing is an added feature worth considering as it enhances the value and quality of the creation of content and the value for these creators of content because companies believe these people to be competent.

It's the last of my list of essential qualities that content writers must possess.

They also have an extensive understanding regarding the English language, or the grammar and language which the writer writes.

It's second, the drive to acquire more knowledge of the subject the writer writes about fourthly, having good reading abilities.

So, let me conclude this discussion here, during this discussion where we talked about our distinct strengths as content writers.

That's all. I'd like to say thank you for your involvement in the course as well as the higher cost on the horizon. We wish you great day and to continue learning.

Chapter 4: Writing By Practice

In the previous presentation we talked about ways to identify if someone is an aptitude for writing one of the most important steps to discover the potential is to begin writing.

The discussion was the fact that it is subjective to write a matter and that the level of popularity of content is a factor which determines its quality.

The discussion also focused on the fact that writing is the most important factor to success at this conference. We'll keep discussing writing skills like we always do.

Let me begin the discussion by saying writing is a process and not a chance, and this is crucial because it is possible to increase the effectiveness of a skill.

Writing is a talent that can be improved and enhance the quality of your writing because you can't learn the ability yourself through practice.

This doesn't mean that everyone has innate ability to write. There are plenty of writers working in the field with natural writing abilities.

If you take a look at the market there are many writers who have developed their writing abilities through the hard work of.

You may be wondering what the reason. What is better than being talented? There's a reason for this. Let me explain.

The writing of marketing content is not an art ... therefore, imagination is essential with a finite availability. Writing content for advertisements is actually technological content creation to get the purpose of attracting attention and interest.

In the race to win. It is commonly utilized by search engines such as Google to win in this particular argument.

As in this case, you can point your content towards the computer programmer, not the capacity of an individual's brain.

To have more success creating content of this kind it is essential to write content that is able to be customized to meet your requirements in accordance with the algorithm of search engines and needs a lot of knowledge.

It doesn't require much talent in the same way like you, as well as writing skills content writer, must possess other abilities to create successful marketing content.

Let me discuss some of these qualities in this presentation. I will discuss them all in a short manner.

Writing skills that are good are essential to create quality content. Simply, it requires writing with precision, clarity and style. These fonts are completely free of lint. A talent to write, naturally it means that you have a knack in the preparation of a skilled writer.

In the beginning, writers should use short words and, as much as possible, less words.

He should stay clear of repetition and unneeded terms and jargon, and the primary characteristic of our Content Writer is the capacity to do research.

You should have a solid background in research, as these are non-fiction works. You will need to do some digging to determine whether you're an experienced or non-expert.

In any subject you must provide your readers accurate details and have the information checked before writing it down. Research is, therefore, a crucial ability required by a successful content writer.

Another aspect is understanding SU. It's normal for a Gordon-Wright to be knowledgeable about this since you had to struggle prior to writing content since SEO is a term used to describe search engine Optimization. It's all about driving visitors to your website from organic or natural sources found on search engines.

It's a waste we'll discuss it at a later moment. Perhaps in a different course.

Being familiar with SEO can be a huge advantage for content writers to write quality content.

Let's examine the next feature that a content writer should keep up-to-date with the latest trends in.

I'm talking about the most recent in his writing about content writers should be active learners when they write on a broad range of subjects.

They should be able to get the most up-to-date information on the subjects they intend to write about so that they can translate complex information into a simple language for readers.

What I'm going to discuss here are the fundamental characteristics required to be an excellent writer. Simply put, the extensive understanding and abilities listed here will answer the question of whether you're able to become a successful author.

Another advantage to creating content for a career is that you are able to select this path regardless of your age. This is a huge benefit to many writers who work in the field currently.

A lot of people have begun working in different areas after having completed their normal years.

They bring with them a lot of experience and knowledge from their previous collaborations and has contributed to this latest lineup.

Many choose to write for a living even at an older age, as long as they have an idea of what they want to do.

The primary discussion is whether or not you have the skills or ability to use writing as a form of expression, and to examine if we must determine if we possess any of these essential traits for being a good content writer. I'll list the qualities on this talk.

Chapter 5: Inspire To Create Content

In the lecture before we examined the characteristics of writing talent.

We talked about how practicing can enhance writing ability and discovered that numerous writers have achieved success with hard work and practice. We have witnessed success creating content. It is important to have these skills.

Along with the caliber of your research, as well as your understanding and the need to stay up to date with the latest developments in the field.

In addition to everything you require to possess a passion for writing, you need to be praised for other important attributes, like an understanding of the grammar of the language along with a keen curiosity and a need for more information about the matter.

All the characteristics you require to be a top-quality content writer.

Let's begin this exciting read, with a lovely quote from the universe.

The court has said that when you make yourself sit down and write then the software will typically be restored.

It is true. I will repeat this fact time and time again throughout the course.

It's only after you begin to write and continue to write and develop the habit of writing you will observe your progress towards becoming an experienced writer.

If you don't attend or stop your writing practice altogether You may not be able to see the improvement you require to enhance your writing abilities. That means your writing ability is always contingent on the speed at which you practice.

If you go through every lecture during this course it will be clear that we typically enjoy two key topics for creating content throughout these lessons.

The first was the reason you needed to become a writer, the other being whether you were a writer or not. Both are essential to create content around these subjects.

In this article, we will discuss an important aspect that influences the process of creating content.

It is an crucial aspect of content creation since it allows us to gain strategies and guidelines to create content.

Let me re-list the most crucial topics of the discussion. In brief, we will look at three major themes that are used to create content for speech.

One of the primary reasons you should consider becoming the content creator is whether or not possess writing abilities. There are three methods to encourage you to write content.

These are the three principal subjects in this program. Learn to use them to be a source of an inspiration for your the creation of content.

It's not as simple a process , as you might imagine since making content is a complicated job.

It's not simple, especially for writers who have just begun writing. If you think that creating content is easy, then you think it is.

It's not so much. It's difficult to find time to write content. It's not an easy undertaking.

The other aspect is that it's difficult to write sentences, paragraphs, and words within our texts that are informative and instruct the reader.

Thus, creating top quality content is an additional process, which is a challenging and original content for an issue is more challenging.

It's an essential task. Making clear content is a challenge in today's world of information, since there's lots of content about a specific topic online. If you decide to write content, you'll be unable to come up with ideas.

Create Unique Content

Making good content can be challenging even for gifted people.

You may have written some great items, excellent content and then when you try to think of an idea that is new but your mind might go completely blank.

This is also a requirement for any professional writer who is a pro. I'll give you the ways to handle this situation, especially those who are struggling with making content.

You'd like to make material for your customers and you're not sure what to do.

There is only one way to conquer your inborn desire to create the creation of content. It is to improve your ability to create content.

Let me begin by highlighting some of these capabilities for you here. These are all abilities that are fundamentally right. I will always write high quality content.

The first and most important thing is that one must have the capacity to conduct extensive studies on a particular topic prior to they can enjoy reading content written by top writers.

This is crucial in the current world of speed and speed in which that time is running out, consequently a captivating title is a great way to draw attention to your blog.

It is important to recognize it is important to consider the caliber of material is attributed to the title must be related to the title, and the content must be excellent to avoid negative reviews about it and the creators of it.

One of the most important abilities for a successful content writer is being capable of distinguishing between the content that is written and regular.

Let me first tell you about the content that was created. When writing content, data about a particular subject or subject is gathered and summarized into an article.

The individuals who carry out this procedure are the ones who have custody of the information contained in the card.

They are always finding groups, and organising and posting some of the best of the latest and relevant online content about a particular topic.

A competent content creator may make use of one or more articles to determine whether an article has been written.

Content writers with a good reputation must be aware of the subject. He is proficient in the language used to convey his message.

They must also know the language of the language in which the article was written.

the topic of discussion in the article, that we've both talked about in past conferences. make content writers feel frustrated by writing stories that are compelling to attract an engaged audience to gather. The concept of storytelling is connected to content marketing today.

In the age of content marketing it's not enough just to produce and publish content. Marketing is about creating a series of experiences. Copywriters make use of content to justify their decisions.

Experiences shared with an audience. In order to accomplish this, you must be precise about the subjects and stories you'd like to share.

The best benefit of using stories to help get your message to your audience is that the content is focused more on the message and experience, and not the format or channel of the message. In addition, the content is developed to fill the gapin in the space of editorial.

This is the final part of this debate. Content writers who are good at their craft must proofread their content that they write.

It is necessary to revise and rewrite your content, and then refine it until it is of your best quality.

We have also talked about this subject in other conference sessions. Let me now summarize some of the issues we've talked about here.

The best writers are able to pick topics that people would like to read.

In this regard, excellent content writers are able to review and search their writing. Research is an essential ability that every content writer must possess.

Sometimes, an author's credibility can be damaged and the whole article gets marginalized. Even if a factual assertion is not true, it can be disastrous. Persistence is a key component of a quality content writers.

It doesn't matter if you're blogging, making content for a website magazine, or creating content for a startup magazine, you will need to be extremely hard at work without getting a lot of credit for your efforts. Therefore, you must do your best.

Be persistent and keep working hard. persevering. To succeed every content writer is experts who write compelling material for their online business which is where internet-savvy is essential.

The majority of content that is created or released via articles, press releases, blog posts, as well as other kinds of material online is currently this presentation and this article.

Chapter 6: Writing Tips For Writing Content

In the last presentation we discussed ways to motivate writers to create fresh original, interesting and relevant content.

We've learned that writing content is not an easy job and creating quality content is a tougher task for a writer.

It was also difficult to come up with unique content and we've seen how.

We've seen that great content is sometimes difficult to write even for an experienced content writer. Therefore, you can imagine how challenging the job is for someone who is novice to creating content.

We will then examine the characteristics of a professional content writer. Let me repeat it to you.

You are extremely crucial. A professional content writer can be expected to conduct thorough research on a certain subject for the creation of content.

A great content writer is able to come up with a brand new title for the content they write that makes it easier to draw attention of the reader to the information.

A competent content writer can differentiate between writing content that is regular and not.

To create better writing, authors create articles that tell stories in order to attract an audience that is engaged. Find content writers who have extensive research skills.

Good content writers possess an grasp of the topic they write about as well as the language they use to create the content. Seven excellent content writers make use of quality in their writing to enhance the quality.

Therefore, we will go over a number of key areas, and help you identify the essential qualities for the growth of a future writer of content.

We'll now move to the brand new call prior to when we get started on the call. I'll give you a brand new heirloom or.

The writing is influenced by Stephen King, and he states that if you wish to become a writer, you need to complete two things to be successful in any task that requires lots of writing and reading. This advice is very useful.

In order to have a cavalry of goodwill for us, we need to learn a lot about the topics that are interesting to us and the subjects we would like to be able to beat, the topics that we'd like to be the best and subjects we'd like to write about.

Your success will be assured when you adhere to these steps. In this presentation I will share some writing tips and inform you something truthfully.

Many of us you will notice when you sit down to write. There's a slight feeling that the material we write isn't the way we would like it to be.

The feeling is a bit nagging us every time we sit to write an advertising copy.

After we had enough experience, we were able to get over this feeling and carried on our efforts to produce content for marketing materials. When we get experience writing, the quality of our work increases significantly.

What I'm trying say is that even if believe that your work isn't quite good enough, don't quit writing.

This is a fundamental principle. If you don't your writing, you'll never be an effective writer.

The loss of writing abilities in these situations is the main reason to put off learning when you write effective content. Your writing will decline at intermediate levels.

If you're trying to be a great journalist, the very first thing you must be able to feel is that you are able to write. Yes, I write, that is your first thought to be able to experience if you are aspiring to become an author.

Keep in mind that this is regardless of your writing abilities. I'm certain that if you believe that you can write, you'll be a better content writer.

If you don't feel this feeling, my advice definitely won't help you and is a waste of your time.

I'm sure you'll thank me for my advice to save time and stop typing. If that's the case or you have any questions, this course will be a great help.

If you're committed to becoming a writer, you're likely to be a successful writer. I would like to inform you that writing content that can assist you in changing your ways or even someone important to your business . It can be very satisfying.

Writing is a talent that is essential throughout all aspects of life, just like any other talent. It takes time to master your writing abilities.

You'll need some instruction and I'll add that you need some direction to help you get out of it in a certain way. Let me share with you my thoughts that these days

Writing content is a great career possibilities if you're proficient and have the capabilities to write.

There is a growing need for skilled content writers. The internet has provided numerous possibilities for writers. there's a lot of income to be made from the field of writing abilities if the content writer is essential as writing is at the core of all forms of writing.

Once you are an expert in content writing, you are able to try different types of writing.

They can provide examples of where you are unable to write creative or technical research, writing and scientific texting, that the wrong people write lots about their trip. There are some who are experts in how to write in the medical area. Medically, you write.

You can make blobs of information with the help of writing essays. There are numerous other possibilities and you'll see that everyone writes in the present.

If you've got a website and you edit it, you're an editor. If you're on social media, make sure you market everything you share.

And Mattie Norris claims that everyone can be an author. Everyone has an email address and Twitter accounts and Facebook pages.

Somehow or other it's how every content creator do it.

Therefore, writing is an art everyone must master, and writing is becoming more crucial because words communicate to our clients who we are.

This can help us appear smart, but it could cause us to be stupid. You must pick the words with care and be sincere with your clients today. Being competent to communicate by yourself isn't enough. It's an absolute requirement.

Let me tell you honestly about the various other content marketing strategies. Writing is one area that has been overlooked but we all are aware that the writing process is the core of every content marketing campaign.

One of my friends once stated the writing process is mix of love and passion. The book is fashionable because it is essential to you and serves a reason for this is because it helps people. Find a equilibrium.

Absolutely true, and the most difficult problem isn't just from your viewpoint of that you can accomplish easily, but rather to write to meet the demands of your readers. You need to write in a way that it's.

Transforms is their thoughts and opinions, as well as their development through their thought processes, and their writings.

This is all there is to this conference. This concludes the lecture, and this course.

I am grateful for you taking the class and allowing me to give my expertise to you should you have any feedback. Make the most of it and find choose the right platform to help you communicate your message.

I would like to encourage you to spend just a few minutes of your time and write a honest rating review to the website.

This will be a an immense boost in the creation of my courses in the future. It's a beautiful day, always learning.

Create exceptional content

If your website isn't equipped with good quality content, it will not be able to serve your visitors, much less your customers. When designing your site, be aware your content as the primary element. Without it your site will be difficult to locate.

A greater quantity of relevant content equates to a higher ranking in search engines. Be sure that the SEO writers are dedicated to making your content unique by adhering to these easy guidelines:

Begin by learning the fundamentals. Make sure to write down your most important points.

You might have shown your skills as a content writer writing a great article about trending summer styles.

If you've neglected to include your store's opening hours in easy to find areas on your site This article will not assist you in any way.

KISS - do it, you're stupid. It's a cliche however one I've discovered applies to a variety of aspects of life and content writing isn't an exception.

More keywords to optimize your search are more effective however this doesn't mean that content creators must spend days, putting in as many keywords as they can.

Make use of your top keywords several times and ensure you weave them into your writing as seamlessly as you can and end the sentence.

Most of the time, ADHD Internet users today don't have the time to read more than few hundred words about any topic.

Create content that is practical. If your reader does not gain anything from reading your article then they will not read it. It's so simple.

As your personal content writer, write about the topic that you are interested in, but be sure that you are taking care of your clients too.

They best SEO writers are able to make the content entertaining and informative, but more important, they are practical.

Be unique. Easy to say but harder to do I'm sure. One of the easiest ways for content creators to be distinctive in their writing is to examine the content of their competitors and determine what's missing.

If you are able to provide details, insights into a debate, news or even entertainment that rivals can't, then you've got an advantage. In addition that you're writing quality original content.

Write Keyword Content

My experience after a few hours online was that the keywords are the lifeblood of the whole system.

This is the reason that I've chosen to focus on this important subject for the contents in this document.

If you decide to make the decision to stay in one place and be successful online, the words will be what it will help you achieve.

You could decide to study copywriting . This is among my best advice for you.

Learn to master words that convince people to do the actions you suggest which is extremely helpful when it comes down to selling. Don't worry about it; I'm not trying sell you anything at this moment.

For success on the internet You must learn to blend two styles of writing which you might not have mastered initially.

It is important to master the art of write with your own voice to be able to connect with your future customers.

You are also required to improve your writing skills to ensure that Google bots and other spiders be able to understand what your content about. Artificial intelligence is a topic that has been discussed before. I bet you didn't think it was possible to achieve this in your own life Did you?

This article we'll discuss how you can write for both audiences and ensure you have the online success we're all seeking.

Many individuals are trying to become rich from their online pursuits while some want to make a comeback from their job, while others want to earn a little extra money to allow them to enjoy a better life. This article focuses on the tools you'll require to accomplish this. The key is to utilize words to achieve your goal This is not a recipe, nor a plan for success.

As a matter of fact, and with some knowledge from my personal experience, can assure your that the keywords serve as the primary starting base for everything that happens online.

If you're not sure the meaning of keywords, they are the terms that people enter into Google's Google Search box. Furthermore the Google search engine will show relevant results from searches by displaying websites that are related to what you're searching for.

If you're a marketer , or webmaster You want your site to be in the initial page Google results for search hoping that the user will visit your website to find what they're searching for.

Each page of search results contains 10 websites, each numbered 1-10 for organic results.

The right side of Google's page are paid or sponsored searches using Google Ad Words and the first three or two results at the top of the page.

The position of the organic results on your page depends of the terms that you select. If you're a novice trying to get noticed for large and competitive terms, then your site is unlikely to show in the first 10 results. it could be hundreds or even thousands of pages hidden in the.

Your website won't not be listed since no searcher will or able to go through many pages of the pages of results to locate you. Therefore, the question becomes how to place your web pages to appear on the first page of Google results for search, preferring to be in the very first result.

In the simplest terms, you have to be aware of the search terms that people looking to discover your business are likely to see on Google's search page or another search engine.

It is possible to begin brainstorming some keywords as if you were the person who searched. This is only the beginning since the search terms will run through your head quickly.

Ideally, you want every page to be optimized to the same keyword or search phrase on your site.

If, for instance, you are able to only think of 50 words, then how can you compare to your competitor who optimizes their website to rank for millions of keywords within your market or niche?

The best option is to make use of a free keyword tool or purchase your own tool for keyword research. If you are serious about marketing, there's no other option.

Each of them has their own tool for keyword research which can generate thousands of keywords that correspond to the specified keyword

Term. In many instances the time savings and mental fatigue can't be quantified in terms of financial.

There are numerous keyword tools are available for download for no cost. One of the best well-known is Google's free keyword tool.

The next keyword tool that is free can be found in Word Tracker. Word Tracker. As you get more familiar with it you may become familiar using Keyword Spy for competitive keyword analysis.

Despite the accessibility of the keywords tools discussed above, many marketers prefer having their own tools for keywords, like Keyword Elite 2.0 or Market Samurai.

They are excellent keywords tools that come with free trials of both and you can test these out before you buy.

This means you'll never take any risk with your own money for for a time. If you're not pleased with the purchase you made and want to return it, you can ask for to refund your purchase within the trial period.

Now that you are aware of the keywords research tools you require and where to purchase they are, you must be able to write the content that is keyword-focused.

As I stated earlier, each article must be identified with keywords.

This means that you need to select a search term for each page and alter the elements on your page to reflect the chosen keyword.

These tools let you write more articles for your website with more keywords.

The majority of free keyword tools will yield a maximum of 100 keywords per keyword.

The keyword should be used throughout your article however, limit the keyword density to 2 to 5 percent per 100 words on the webpage.

In the title, your piece must include your key words or keywords in the first paragraph in the name.

You can incorporate your keywords to create Google Ad campaigns and ads which target the products you're selling on your site.

But, you shouldn't bombard other websites with your keyword e.g. B. Web 2.0 properties , or bookmarks on websites that promote your site.

The aim in the final analysis is attract as many people as you can to your website , so they are able to purchase what you sell.

When the issue with traffic is solved, the next task is to convert those sales into traffic and I'll cover this in a different article.

Be sure to utilize one of the paid-for keyword tools that were mentioned earlier to place serious internet experts and marketers on the same playing field.

They utilize both free and paid keywords tools to conduct their keyword research, as do you.

Chapter 7: What To Beware Of When Creating Content For Websites

In this day and age, where every company and business is trying to boost sales and pay focus on their online marketing strategy you don't want to have poor web content.

This can only happen it your visitors become leads after having read captivating content on your website.

The content on your website determines the accessibility of your site to the general public.

The creation of content for websites is an activity that requires a catalyst to achieve successful outcomes.

It is therefore important to be worried about the content on your site. Here are a few points to keep in mind when making website content:

Research on the internet has revealed some interesting facts about online readers.

The majority of the visitors to your site are the younger age group. They are extremely impatient and don't wish to spend long hours on one particular site.

Insane and boring content frustrates users very quickly. Design your website's content by analysing these elements.

Your content must be brief useful, informative, and timely. To drive sales, focus on engaging and captivating web-based content.

As you may have guessed that the world of the web is comprised of people from all walks of life Many of them are educated, while others are not so well-educated.

Take note of this idea and develop your website's content in line with this. Choose simple words and concise sentences.

Be sure that the flow of speech stays constant throughout your text. Making content for a website is an effective task in which imagination and skills are balanced by optimizing and creating accessible content.

Beware of using informal language on your site's content because this can seriously impact the potential for branding promotion.

When you write material for your website be aware the fact that you're acting on behalf of the authoritative authority.

If a visitor gets an indication that you're inflicting false information on them and they quit your site immediately.

Thus, only purchase genuine and authentic data. This can also result in your online business being successful.

In the online world there are thousands of websites being added each day. It is becoming more difficult for users to remember URLs of websites.

They make use of search engines to locate the website that is targeted.

It is therefore essential to improve search engine ranking by incorporating appropriate keywords in website content.

Be extremely specific in regards to the amount and position of keywords in the content of your website. Artificial keywords should be natural.

By incorporating these suggestions to your website, you will be able to make your website more appealing and gain an advantage over your competitors.

Important skills

The way a web content writer puts keywords on a web page could be as crucial just as keywords in themselves.

When you've compiled your list of top keywords Do not just smear your keywords across the web as an Easter-themed brush. Incorrect use of keywords could render them ineffective or unusable.

There are three key ideas that every content writer must be aware of when it comes to keywords.

The degree of compliance with terms is largely dependent on the way a website reacts to search engines, such as Google, Bing, and Yahoo! belongs.

Select at least one sentence per page.

Content writers must optimize every page for at least two keywords. Optimizing a website for several keywords is difficult since the best places for keywords are all on the same page.

The position that is restricted like the beginning of a tag need to remain reserved to the primary keyword.

Secondary keywords (words that are less significant than those of) are then used to complement the primary keyword.

If you are using the primary keyword once every 100 words or less then you're using about only half of the secondary keyword.

Check the Density

The frequency with which a content writer adds a keyword to an article in relation to the number of words that appear on the page can have an enormous impact on the website's position in search results.

If a user is searching for a particular keyword the search engine scans the page for density, which is the ratio of the search phrase to the total terms on the webpage.

When the content density excessive such as 50 percent the search engine could determine that the site was made solely to attract interest of the engine. In the event that density not high enough the search engine could be unable to read the content completely.

Include keywords on your website

If a writer of content for a website produces multiple pages using the word or keyword in it, it is much more likely that the site will be ranked higher on an engine search than a single-page website that contains the key word or keyword.

Some search engines, such as Google and others, will show two results on a page (one with an indentation below one). If your site has only one page for the keyword however, it may not be.

What exactly is SEO content?

Search engine friendly (SEO) content refers to the kind that engines search for.

The more engaging and well-written the SEO content on your site the more beneficial your site will be for your clients and the better it will appear in top ranking of search engines.

Search engines such as Google are quite intelligent - they are able to not only detect any content that you have posted, but assess its quality and accessibility.

If your website's content isn't SEO-friendly, then search engines will not perform as well.

Search engine optimization isn't only about using more keywords is possible.

Google doesn't look up this kind of content. Neither do your customers.

Your customers are looking for information They want to be entertained , or they are looking for the most recent information about what's happening in your area.

Repeatedly repeating "trendy shoes" will not get them anywhere.

If you're planning to function in the role of SEO Content Writer here are some useful guidelines to make your content as user-friendly and user-friendly as is possible.

* Choose the terms and keywords that are directly connected in your industry. If your offerings don't align with the SEO contents, prospective customers won't be loyal to your brand for very long.

* Use three to four keywords for each 400-word article. Try using each of these words twice within 400-words.

If you use your keywords in too many places, it will make your content more difficult to read and cause readers to lose focus.

If you do not use your keywords properly your search engine visibility major search engines could be affected.

* Use your keywords as effortlessly as is possible. Don't try to insert keywords into places in which they don't belong.

* Write about subjects that could be interesting to your customers. You might want to consider adding a blog on your website , so that you are able to regularly add articles that are SEO-friendly and keep your visitors returning to read more.

Use the Google Keyword Tool to choose the best words for your website.

Utilize Keywords when writing SEO Content

Setting up a website may be simple, but gaining and maintaining that rank on search engines isn't an easy feat.

The rank of a site is determined by the SEO content it contains. It was discovered that a lot of websites suffered from a drop in rankings. They eventually declined due to holes on their pages' content.

Writing content to use for SEO is different than writing. You must consider the appropriate search engine optimization, maintain freshness, keep content updated regularly , and keep it informative.

It's only if Internet visitors find content fascinating and unique that they continue to visit the website. This ensures the highest site traffic.

The process of writing content to be used for SEO concerns the proper use and positioning of keywords. If you are planning to write material for your website make sure you research keywords meticulously.

You can seek help with tools like good keyword and word trackers. By following this method, it will help you to identify the importance of keywords and the most frequently used keywords for research.

After you've selected your keywords, conduct the search and you will be amazed at the number of search results indexed when you type in the keywords.

It's always best for you to keep an eye on the opposition your site will be facing as you write SEO-related content.

When you are writing content to use for SEO Avoid clogging the content with similar keywords.

In the past, incompetent content writers believed that using the same keywords would aid in ranking higher and draw in more visitors. But the landscape has changed over the years.

The search engines employ certain algorithms, which could easily detect this method as a mistake and your site will be penalized right away.

Instead of using keywords that are generic and phrases, use keywords or phrases that can bring in more traffic. If the content that is used for SEO includes a number of terms, it may influence the search engine's ranking and also the web traffic.

Always separate keywords using the use of a punctuation mark. Without a comma search engine will mark each keyword as lengthy sentences.

SEO content can only be appreciated and read by people in the event that the keywords are put in prominent locations and are of a certain density.

A skilled writer selects the appropriate keywords that are in line with the content. It's possible to say that creating SEO content is an easy and challenging task. If your website does not meet certain standards, it rapidly affects the ranking of your site.

You must be professional and produce unique and original content that draws ever more people to your site.

Chapter 8: Developing Your Content Marketing Strategy

One of the most effective instruments you can incorporate into your marketing plan is the use of content marketing. Content marketing can be used to make you an expert in your field and leads to the growth of your business's revenues, while also being a lucrative source of income. But, producing content that will help you build your following and build a profitable business isn't a quick growth strategy. It takes a long time for your content to become a success.

Before you start creating content for your company You must be clear about your business objectives in order to create an effective marketing plan. This is particularly true with regards to content marketing. It is vital to maintain a consistent method in your content that you're creating. A regular approach provides you with information that keeps your customers active, leading to them considering you to be an authority in the field. If your company is perceived as an authority in a particular area and your customers are more likely to buy from you at the moment that is appropriate.

To ensure that your company can realize a profit for your content marketing investment it is crucial to create a complete system that is built around your main content platform. A comprehensive system will allow you to make use of your resources and help increase your revenue instead of wasting your money. In order to run an effective content marketing strategy It is crucial to view your complete approach to marketing through content in a system that makes your content dynamic and where your audience is engaged at every step.

The Content Marketing Ecosystem

The strategy for content you initially develop will expand and develop. In order for your strategy to be efficient and healthy it must incorporate various components. There are two kinds of content must be considered in establishing your strategy. regular content and content assets. Recurring content builds your client database over time whereas content assets can be used to help you acquire clients in the near future. tool.

When you are working with an ongoing system there are six components that must be taken into consideration to maintain the health of the ecosystem

* Front-end content of high-quality.
* An opt-in deal
* A sequence of emails to be onboarding
* An initial conversion possibility
* A sequence of follow-ups
* Another opportunity to convert

The asset system is comprised of four components and is able to be used as a stand-alone system or with the regular system. The four components required for the asset system to function are as follows:

* A high-quality , long-form content asset
* An initial engagement opportunity
* A first conversion opportunity
* A follow-up email sequence

Here's a brief review of the components you must include in both your recurring content systems as well as the system for content assets.

It is comprised of six parts: the Recurring Content Ecosystem

Top-Quality Front End Content

Although it may sound simple, the content you produce for your company should be top-quality. It must be entertaining as well as informative and practical. It should be a valuable resource for both you and your clients. It is essential to accurately format your text and make sure that it is spell-checked prior to publishing it online. Establish a routine for publishing your content. This will offer the best details about your business regularly.

Make an opt-in offer

Regularly publishing content on a regular time frame will drive visitors to your website. But, when the visitors have completed the content then they'll leave. A opt-in deal will track that traffic and you will be able to engage them even after they leave your website. Opt-in deals typically come in the form of a pop-up , or an online form which will offer an asset with an email address in exchange. Opt-in offers that are effective include reports on industry trends white papers cheat sheets educational courses checklists coupons webinars, video lessons or downloads/demos.

A sequence of emails to be onboarding

Once you have enlisted a lead through your opt-in-to-opt-in campaign After capturing a lead, you must take them onboard with a series consisting of emails sent automatically. It typically consists of between four and eight emails that inform the reader about your business and provides some of your organization's best sources, and then encourages the subscriber to join your organization. This component of the system engages them on a deeper level, and boosts their trust in your company's image, and also sets the expectations for their future interactions with you.

An Initial Conversion Opportunity

After nurturing your leads with your email sequence, giving them useful details and offering your knowledge and knowledge, it's now time to make an offer. The previous interactions you've had with them should have naturally led you to this point, so that the customer is happy with your offer and ready to accept the offer.

A Follow-up Sequence

Your initial proposal could result in two different groups created that have converted, and those that didn't. It is crucial to follow up to both of these groups. If you follow up with the ones who actually took up your offer , you must a) give them an upgrade or upsell and then) taken on board to maximize the value of the products they've purchased. For those who weren't convinced, you must a) give them a discount

A light or sell version of your original offer in order to test to convert them and b) integrate them in a new sequence that provides customers with additional knowledge and help to help them prepare for the next offer.

Another Conversion Opportunity

In the time you spend with each client You'll want to offer a variety of offers. It's easier to keep a customer than to acquire a new one. That's why it is important to create a variety of systems that will allow you to increase the value of every customer. If you decide to set up the automated sequence of emails or start new cycles, it's vital to have a recurring sales process in place.

A Four-Part Asset Ecosystem

A high-quality long-form content asset

Webinar series, books Web summits, books, and videos that are multi-part can all be content assets. For the majority of businesses books are the best choice, since the printed copies is a actual calling cards. They can be mailed to prospective customers and turn their potential into bigger opportunities for your company. This may include interviews as well as speaking engagements.

An Initial Engagement Opportunity

This section of the ecosystem is sending out an invitation to your prospective customers to join you on call, attend an event, webinar, or get a demo for your service. It is important to offer the next step that you would like to offer your prospect after they've been connected to your asset, which gives them a live or one-on-one conversation with your company.

An Initial Conversion Opportunity

The first conversion opportunity is to simply make an offer in the initial interaction with the potential customer. When you're presenting the web or in a webinar, or speaking to them via the phone, you must to take advantage of this opportunity to ask them to act by presenting an offer that is specific to them.

The Follow-Up email sequence

As in the recurring system the follow-up emails sequence is designed to divide prospects into two categories that do not convert, and those who convert. It is also necessary to follow up with each of the groups. In one email sequence you can onboard new customers and sell the products you offer and services, while the second series will be resold and inserted into a separate sequence, which makes them more receptive to your next promotion.

It's essential that you establish an established guiding principle that guides every marketing effort of your business. This will be the basis for your decisions and helps you focus on the right issues.

Chapter 9: Finding Your Audience

Successful copywriting campaigns have three aspects. In the first place, you must identify the ideal market. Once you've established your intended audience, you'll need to create the perfect offer and lastly, you'll must write the perfect copy. Three elements are essential if would like your content marketing strategy to succeed. It is possible to engage the best copywriter but if you're not reaching the right people or are offering mediocre content your efforts in your content will be in vain.

To develop a successful marketing strategy, it is essential an in-depth understanding of your target audience. You must focus your efforts on content that is evergreen that is valuable throughout time and remains relevant to your target audience. Although you may have an notion of who your people are, you do not have a specific persona to build an effective campaign around. That's why it's important for your company to create an avatar of the customer.

Why you need a Customer Avatar

In the past few years, the idea of an avatar for customers has gained momentum. Achieving a user avatar helps you to gain a better understanding of the motivations of your customer and desires, as well as fears and issues that affect their buying choices. Making a profile that reveals the priorities, issues and objectives, allows you to personalize your marketing strategy to meet your customers best.

Every business is able to serve many different customers and customers, having a persona for your customer will allow you to identify your most important customers, those who are for whom your product is an easy choice. When you are deciding if a particular market segment is the best one for your company You must take an all-encompassing approach and look at perspectives, capabilities, and the potential for profit.

Looking at Perspective

It is about making sure that your customers' behavior is similar to your own. It is your goal to ensure that they share the same values in their priorities, goals, and orientation towards your company. It is vital that the viewpoints of your customers and your company are aligned.

Examining the capabilities

It's about your company's embedded resources. This is the resource and assets that allow your company to service customers of a certain type better than a different. The most important aspect of choosing the appropriate audience is to determine whether your abilities are in line to the customer's needs and potential.

Examining the potential for profit

In assessing the potential profit of the market you are considering when assessing the potential profit of your chosen market, you must consider the following questions:

* Does your target audience have a budget that will allow your costs?

* Does your service promise result in a significant profit, which makes it a no-brainer for them to work with you?

* Do you have to expand your product or services in order to increase your margins on profit?

Examining those three categories will give you the theoretical framework to understand the type of people you want to reach. The next step is to create an avatar for your customer that represents your group of customers. When you are creating your avatar for your customer You must consider the following.

* Age
* Gender
* Income
* Family status
* Location
* What they are looking for
* What they strive for
* Fears
* Frustrations
* Challenges
* Likes
* Do not like
* What they've read
* Their habits on social media.
* How do they can relax

Chapter 10: To Make The Best Offers

Once you've established who your intended audience is The next step in your content marketing strategy is to make sure that you're making the appropriate offerings. The services and products you provide should be tailored to the needs of your main clients. Your

Your primary customers are what matters most. Now having taken your time identifying your customers, it's time to provide them with the things they need.

To determine the types of offers that are most likely to succeed in your industry it is necessary to revisit and look at your main customers. You need to know what they require to know, their needs, their challenges and their motives so that you can find the best offers you can offer them. There's a certain amount in trial-and-error in the process of determining the best deals and it may take a while for the right offer to be realized. It's possible that you create a variety of offers which will appeal to your market. To select the most effective offer you should be aware of what is most important to your customers. To identify the most valuable product to them, you need to know the needs of your intended audience.

Making the Right Offer

The process of developing a product takes a lot of time regardless of whether you're developing an online course, physical product or consulting service. A single of the most important things you can do to improve your business is to create the best products. Your company is built upon the products you offer your customers , and just making something up to create products to sell is not the method to expand your company. Market validation is crucial to designing the best products to your intended customers. Before you begin designing your offer, it's crucial to follow these essential steps.

Get the facts

Although you may have an idea of the issues your clients are facing and the solutions they're looking for, you'll need to talk to your customers to better understand what they want from you. This can be accomplished in many different methods. Start by observing the people and asking them questions to help quickly assess whether your assumptions are correct. This can aid in determining if they use your service or product in the manner you believe they should and what it does for them.

To verify whether your assumptions regarding your customers are true You can ask them these questions.

* Why did you decide to utilize this product/service?

How do you use this product or the service?

• What's the most important issue that it will solve for you?

* What are the secondary issues it can solve for you?

Has it made your life simpler? How?

* What do like best regarding it? Do you have anything you'd like to like to change?

* Did you look at alternatives? What was the reason you chose our solution?

Do you have any concerns or doubts? Have you had any questions that weren't answered?

* Do you have any other suggestions you think we should be doing?

If you're a brand new business and don't have a client base, you could be in touch with people who are in line with your primary customer profile and then reframe your concerns around a potential product or service you're considering providing.

Simplify

Always strive at simplicity. If you're not able to communicate what you're providing in just two or three sentences, it's too complex and won't attract an interest from your most important clients. You should be able to explain your solution for their needs quickly. The more complex something appears to be, the less likely your customer will pay the attention. It's human nature to search for the shortest route. Humans do not like handling things that demand the most of our time, so be cautious and use prudential and provide your customers with an easy experience.

Review

Always keep an eye on your offerings. It's normal that your market will shift. To stay in business it is essential to be able to adapt to those shifts. One of the most detrimental ways to harm your company is to embrace the "set and forget" attitude. It is important to be aware that your job isn't finished when you decide on a particular product and customers. There are many things that can alter what your intended audience and requires, which is why it is crucial to examine your offerings frequently.

Small adjustments to your business are as effective as big ones. It is important to take an inventory of your market and the products you have to offer in order to spot these shifts. Although it can be challenging to be impartial about your business, being attentive to the opinions of your customers is crucial to the success of your company.

Chapter 11: Making Your Content

After you've identified your customers, you've determined your message and offer message, you're now ready to begin working on your actual content. Before you start you must create your channel plan in order to define precisely the platforms you'll use to publish your material once it's finished. The plan should outline the platforms you'll be using to present your story, the requirements, your process and goals for each piece of content that you create. Also, you should include the way you plan to connect every piece of content to build a brand-wide conversation.

When you're ready to begin making your content, remember that whatever you write for your business should be centered on the five pillars listed below.

The Five Pillars of Content Creation
Simplicity

The level of complexity of the topic will determine the way an article will be able to perform. If you're unable to distill the subject into something that is simple and easy to comprehend and understand, then it should not be utilized. Although there are concepts that are complicated and require extensive analysis and exploration of the technical aspects It is important to tackle those subjects in a straightforward manner. That's the sole way you can guarantee your audience returns to your website.

Specificity

Specificity is closely tied to the simplicity of your content is self-selecting for your audience. If you do it right your visitors will return to your site to find specific solutions. When writing your content you must think about these questions.

Who reads the text?

* What is the particular issue they're trying to solve?

What is the greater order outcome they're trying to attain?

* What is the specific solution that you could offer that will help them get this goal?

Serendipity

Sometime, subjects will fall in your laps, and you must be ready to grab the opportunity to grab them right away. While it is important to establish an editorial calendar but you must also be able to modify the schedule quickly in the event of a change. It is possible that you will be able to interview someone extraordinary and then publish the interview prior to your competitor gets the chance or your business might be featured in a publication which gives you the opportunity to propel the pace as much as you could. It is crucial to recognize that opportunities like this occur frequently. It is vital to be aware of the events in the world around you and make use of these opportunities, rather than letting chance to pass you by.

Discipline

If you're hard at work, it's an ability to show up more frequently. Becoming disciplined in the production of high-quality content will provide you with the opportunities of high-quality that your business requires to be successful. One of the biggest challenges entrepreneurs face is finding time to write the content. Content will only be effective when you're constant. It's essential to publish regularly in order to get the maximum advantages from your marketing content plan. If you aren't able to commit to creating content on your own and you're not able to do it yourself, you should get someone else to manage it on your behalf.

If you decide to write your own content then you must choose ideas that are inspiring to you. This is crucial because , no matter you're an extremely disciplined individual you know If you find boring content it won't be a good idea writing about it. Only ideas that are exciting will inspire you enough to stick to your writing schedule.

Content Delegation

The ability to be disciplined to do the job, doesn't mean you need to take on the entire task. As the head of your company, generating content might just not be the best way to use the time you have, even though you have themes that interest you.

Finding someone who can assist in the creation of content is a powerful factor that you could create. This is particularly true if you are hiring someone with written experience.

Making Recurring Content

The content you produce regularly like blogs, YouTube videos, and podcasts are what people view as content marketing. However, many business owners confuse publishing content as marketing. Writing lots of content will not ensure that you'll make profits. If you don't have a strategy that includes the collection of emails and sending out onboarding or follow-up material, and offering sales-specific offers, you'll never build an established following or make money. To convert customers you must make sales pitches, regardless of what type of marketing strategy you're using.

If you are in the business of producing regular content, you need to determine the best way to achieve your objectives while remaining inspired to create content regularly. To create a strategy for marketing that is beneficial to your company it is essential to think about these questions.

* What's the objective to our business?

* Who is the target audience we're trying be able to reach?

What kinds of marketing strategies should we employ? Are we using the right type of content for our company?

* Is there anyone within the company who can make the material?

* What is the topic we should concentrate on?

Is our audience attracted to this type of content?

* What other forms of marketing strategies should we employ to ensure that our content is performing for us?

* How can we gauge the effectiveness in our marketing content plan?

In order to create content that can draw interest of the customers and turn the attention into actual sales conversions, you must to offer the possibility of conversion. The content you create must create a scenario in which your target audience has the chance to convert the offer they received at the beginning of the relationship. This can be converted to a different price .

the roadand introduce people to your company which will convert.

Selecting Your Front-End Content Themes

Content is most likely to be successful best in the event that it's released regularly. Some businesses feel that posting every week a few times is sufficient for them, while other businesses using social media, have found that posting many posts every day is sufficient for them. However, many businesses are struggling to produce content consistently due to a lack of knowledge about the subjects they should cover. This can be incredibly demoralizing since you've not only lost your energy and missed out on a important marketing opportunity, but you've failed to communicate to your target audience and thereby tarnish your credibility.

One method to avoid getting in this trap is to look through your customer service documents and review your interactions with potential customers. Find the most frequently asked queries that are asked, and what topics you are constantly required to discuss. Think about what you would like to be recognized for, and what your customers expect from you and identify your distinctive marketing strategy. By analyzing this information you'll be able to develop three to four general concepts that you can review repeatedly from various perspectives.

In each of these areas is a great opportunity to create a multitude of subtopics that you can write on in weekly posts. Begin at the beginning of each quarter to determine three to four subtopics you could write about in the context of the themes you've already determined. It is important to come up with some headline ideas for each topic, as well as up to five important aspects to be addressed in each article. Make a spreadsheet with this information as well as an approximate publication schedule.

This will let you take a seat and write good content each week effortlessly. A strategy is the simplest way to achieve this since you won't need to worry about deciding on an idea or coming up with talk points or fighting writer's blocks. The hardest part.

In addition to creating a few of topics that are regular You will also need to create an outline of topics that you will revisit that you could discuss time. You should plan to cover all of your main themes every month, along with one of your other subjects each week for six weeks. This will position you as an expert in the field.

Make an Opt-In-Offer

Content by itself isn't enough. To establish a connection with your readers and customers, you must discover a method of communication with them regularly. It isn't a guarantee that your visitors will be able to visit your blog regularly or make purchases from you on their own.

In the current world of information it's difficult for anyone to discern what's good and what's useful. The modern consumer is in desperate need of transparency and confidence in their interactions, including those with businesses. Your content, when combined with your ongoing communications with your customers, gives you the best chance to provide customers with confidence and the transparency they want.

The majority of content you'll be creating will be distributed through platforms that you do not own such as Facebook, Twitter, search engines and content networks. These platforms are the ones that control traffic and if they make changes to their business practices there is a chance to lose your followers. This is why creating your own contact list of people you own is essential. This is where opt-in deals can be of use.

When a new customer visits your site, there ought to be an opportunity to invite them to sign up for your mailing list as an incentive. Inquiring about their email address or allowing them to create an account is essential to create their profile, connect with them and then create a specific sales offers to email your contacts when the time is appropriate.

The opt-in deals you offer do not have to be difficult. When you've created a fantastic piece of content that provides important information, don't hesitate to release it. Each day that you do not provide an opt-in option that is active is a day you're losing leads and are wasting your time. Although you should give your customers an exclusive piece of content, at minimum you must include a pop-up which asks for their email address.

Develop an Onboarding Sequence

The process of getting an individual to supply you with their email address, or getting them to open an account with your business is a major win. This is the first step in obtaining their consent to buy something from you and also obtaining their consent to directly market to them directly. This is a major deal and you'll need to make the most of the potential.

A sequence of emails onboarding is designed to open a door for you to directly market to potential customers. The majority of onboarding sequences comprise between four and eight emails that teach your customers about your business, allow you to interact with your community on the internet and are infused with your ideals. The purpose for the series is to position you as an authority in the that they have opted to learn about and convince them to move to an action.

Whatever your next interaction with the potential customer crucial to ensure that you're putting the customer to be in contact with you. Don't assume that your prospect will go through every piece of information you offer and decide to contact with you or even buy something. You must ensure there is something specific that you're leading your customers towards. It is crucial to ensure that your customers are not uncertain of what they need to do next. This is the case throughout the course of the subscription as it goes through your network and is particularly relevant in this particular stage.

Every piece of content you create to date in your content marketing plan is supposed to lead the prospective customer to engage in a live-streamed conversation with your company. Always push your prospects towards some form of interaction with your business. The most crucial aspect of content that converts well is to have an explicit call to action to move your potential client through the sales funnel.

Make Sales Offers

To make content that is converting the audience, you must have the right conversion point. In spite of the advances that have been made in the field of marketing but you have to prepare a sales proposal to convert potential customers. There isn't any way to get the sale without first making an offer to sell.

All businesses are dependent on the volume of sales they can make. The quality of your system not important, nor is having a strong team If you're not able to make an offer for sales that you can't close any sales. You must be committed to completing the sale, that's why you need to be able ignore the fear of being rejected and your fear of offending people, and even the voice saying you're not capable of doing it.

Offers for sales come in all sizes and shapes. Whatever you offer you are offering, make sure to clearly state that you will offer your customer the product or service you offer in exchange for a specified amount. If you're afraid of making sales-related offers on the side of your content or you make an ill-informed attempt to sell your product without demonstrating to the customer the advantages of your product or service, your content won't make a difference to a single client making you waste your money and time and ultimately leading to the loss of your company.

One of the best advantages of the content ecosystem is that the majority the people you meet will already be potential customers, meaning it is more probable respond positively to your offers.

Follow-up with your Prospects

It's not often that you'll get an initial conversion when you get in touch with your potential customer. If your onboarding funnel starts doing its task of bringing them into your company and demonstrating your worth, you could get a fairly high conversion rate right from the beginning. However, for the majority of businesses getting to the point of conversion may be a matter of a few conversations.

People are now more interested in knowing that you're a reliable and legitimate company and that there are other businesses that have worked successfully with them. If your customers have been through the entire system, they'll know you, trust and appreciate your company, and know the benefits of the services you provide. If they haven't been converted and they're not satisfied, you need to introduce the follow-up method to life.

If you're not able to convert them from prospect into a buyer within the first meeting it is important to follow-up with them within two weeks. It is crucial to keep in touch with them on time and reiterate the reason for contacting your company, including how you can aid them. Prepare to address any additional questions they may have, and address those issues they've discussed with you, while proving the reasons why you're a good partner. If someone expressly states that they don't like what you have to offer and isn't interested in talking with you it is important to keep in touch with them.

Making Content Assets for Your Content

To prove that you're an authority and possess a unique depth of expertise in your field It is essential to create content assets. Content assets are lengthy documents that are able to be used to draw in high-end customers. The best method to put your business noticed by large clients is to offer your knowledge in a transparent and generous manner.

The creation of a strategy around content assets is not a good idea for every business. For instance, companies that sell e-commerce will be better off constructing their content marketing strategies that revolves around regular content. This is also true for companies that sell products with a low price point. But, companies that offer premium products or services will gain by establishing a plan built around content assets as they can be a convincing proof of authority and trustworthiness.

Content assets are a great way to improve your recurring content. In contrast to recurring content that places your brand in front of an audience of many Content assets elevate your business above the businesses that compete in your field. It demonstrates that you are dedicated to your field and that you are an expert with real knowledge and resources, while also acting as a badge of honor and establishing your company from competitors.

Get Your Concept Clear

The first step to creating content assets is to clarify your idea. No matter if you choose to create your own content or hire a professional to do it You must have a clear idea in the mind.

Make an outline

Once you've identified your subject then you'll need to develop an outline that outlines the subject matter you'd like to speak about. The basis of creating an asset of content is an extensive outline that covers all the components required for a client to be converted. This is the guideline for the entire process of creation.

Making a thorough sketch of what you intend to write can ensure that you've got all the necessary information and you don't have to be concerned whether you've missed something. It will let you see the exact location you're throughout the process of creating your content and how much remains to be completed, and what things must be changed in order to make sense for the user.

Making the Content

Once you've finished creating your outline, it's time to record your thoughts on each of the points you've listed. Keep each time slot to not more than one hour so that you do not become exhausted and resulting in lower motivation. If you are tired, it can be a problem.

Once you've sorted out the key points of your outline, it's now time to begin transcribing your notes as well as adding sources and information as required. This method lets you capture all your unique insights as well as your expertise and point of view without the need for a long time commitment.

After you've completed the transcription of all the recordings, you're now able to begin your editing. Look for three or four people who are comfortable with the subject matter, and request them to go through the content. Make them search for grammatical and spelling mistakes, as well as structural issues such as the absence of details. Give them two weeks to read through the content, then review it, and make any changes or suggestions you think are appropriate when compared with the original idea of the material.

Leveraging the Asset

This involves creating excitement about the asset that you've created, and then building followers with your targeted group of people. You'll need to start marketing your asset while it's being developed. It's not a good idea to be waiting until it's finished before you begin to promote your customers. Make use of this time to set up guest blogs as well as giveaways, interviews on podcasts and launch events to help build the date of launch.

A Note on SEO

A well-thought out SEO strategy is vital to ensure that your content to rank highly on search engines. The higher your content's rank the more likely it is to be discovered by the appropriate people. When you think about SEO there are three principles that you should be aware of.

* Search engines aim to answer queries of users and earn profits in the process.

The search engines have more knowledge about their workings than any SEO specialist

* Search engines can modify any ranking technique and can punish you for using it.

When writing SEO content, it's crucial to keep a main keyword in mind when writing. It is also essential to include the keyword phrase repeatedly throughout the content. When you are deciding on the keywords you will use should you aim at ones with the monthly search volume less than 10,000 and that are not a lot of competition. These numbers can be found using Google's Google Keyword Planner tool within Google AdWords.

When you start creating your content, make sure to be aware of these five fundamental principles to use when creating content that is SEO-friendly.

Please answer the questions.

* Give the best answer to the question.

* Give a complete response to the question

* Make it a reality

* Over-deliver

SEO is a proven method to boost your business' standing when prospective customers search for certain keywords. If you want your content to be effective, it requires more than just creating a website that is keyword-rich it is essential to incorporate it into your overall marketing strategy.

Chapter 12: Disseminating Your Content

Making a strategy for content marketing that generates conversions is heavily dependent on a continuous flow of eyes that are constantly looking over your content. If you've implemented a recurring strategy or one that is asset-driven it is unlikely to make an ounce if nobody is able to see it, no matter how amazing the content. If you want to get people to interact with your content, you need to be proactive about the way you distribute it.

Email Marketing

Email marketing remains among the top effective strategies to make the most the content you create. It's always the easiest way for companies to reach their customers. It's the sole distribution channel that directly to the audience and is the only one customized to the individual's name, desires, and purchases from the past.

There are three kinds of email campaigns can be used for your business: the welcome campaign, the lead nurture campaigns, as well as offers campaign. Each type of campaign has a specific objective. The welcome campaign was designed to be immediate

Engage your customers and inform them that you'll be in contact with them. The lead nurture program is created to help your target audience discover your company and establish confidence in your brand. The offer campaign is designed to present them with pertinent, timely sales promotions.

Utilizing Social Media

With the increasing popularity of social media platforms increasing they have become a vital instrument for businesses to get their content seen by the appropriate people. Because potential customers are engaging on social media with companies, it's an excellent method of distributing your content to as many people as you can. Effective social media marketing could help your business achieve remarkable growth while forming loyal brand advocates , and increasing leads and sales.

Each social media platform has its advantages, benefits, style of communication and obstacles. Choosing which one works best for you is contingent on the type of audience you're seeking to connect with, the type of content you're producing, and the objectives you're trying to reach.

Facebook

Facebook remains the best platform for building personal connections with your customers according to their interests. It's got a large audience and an almost universal popularity, making it an easy component of your content marketing plan.

Twitter

Twitter boasts more than 334 million active users each month and is the most popular of micro-marketing. It has rapidly become the most popular social network for those who want to be informed and to discuss the events in their lives at the particular moment. Businesses can utilize it to increase the impact of their long-form content by tweeting the most important takeaway and links to the complete article.

YouTube

Videos uploaded to YouTube receive millions of views each day, making YouTube the most popular for sharing videos. YouTube videos are widely appealing and emotionally powerful, which makes videos a fantastic method to create unique, exciting, and immersive experiences that help increase brand awareness while also achieving other top of the line marketing goals.

Instagram

Instagram is a social media platform that has taken the content-based micro-conversations that helped make Twitter an international sensation as well as added an artistic twist. It's the ideal platform for companies to capture genuine moments that add a sense of the human element to their product.

Pinterest

Pinterest is now the largest online scrapbook in the world that transforms content into a easily catalogued art form. It is a great platform for discovering content and is now a favorite among B2C marketers, who want to convert window shoppers into educated consumers by sharing their own passions.

LinkedIn

LinkedIn has been regarded for a long time as the standard for professional networking. Since the launch of its Publisher program that allowed users to create personal content on the site, LinkedIn started to gain recognition as a viable instrument for businesses. Businesses now utilize the platform to increase their

influence and thought-leadership, to help support their content published in other platforms and to spread the opportunities for work they provide.

Google+

Anyone with any Google product such as Gmail drive, Gmail or analytics can access their private Google+ account. This makes Google+ an extremely broad, task-oriented alternatives to the other platforms for social networking. It's a fantastic method of generating brand awareness, to share deep details about the industry, and also for increasing brand influence.

Utilizing social media platforms to share the content of your business is essential for companies today. Every platform has its advantages and advantages, and it's the responsibility of businesses to decide which will be the best to distribute their content to their followers.

Chapter 13: A Writer's Box

If you visit an engineer or a doctor, there is no need to be told that they are one, and this is because his appearance is enough to convey the message. Although he might have the required skills to perform his professional tasks What gives you more confidence in his abilities are the tools he uses. Imagine a doctor is able the treatment of a person suffering from high blood pressure, but not having the BP testing kit. Even although he's qualified however, his precision and accuracy is likely to be affected.

Like every other profession writing is one of them but not all are yet to acknowledge it as it is. If you want to write with ease and achieve recognition, you have to be equipped with the proper tools. If, for whatever reason, you're in a position to pay for expensive electronic writing tools such as an livescribe pen, everlast notebook and idea paint and so on. There are nevertheless, a few basic tools that shouldn't be missing from your collection.

You're only as good as the tools you use and, when you have the right tools, your writing experience will be simple.

It's impossible to compare a farm operation with the hoe with that of the tractor. The latter is more efficient, less stressful , and is always more productive.

As a writer that needs to write blog posts, articles, and social media content or even blog on a daily basis It is essential to be able to have certain tasks automatized. This will allow you to concentrate more on writing content and less on proofreading or editing. With the proper tools, self-repetition can be prevented.

This chapter will present proper tools in the form of applications and software , and the reasons why they shouldn't ever be lacking in your writing catalog as writer.

1. Tools for Editing and Writing

They are a tool to type and edit and also for the identification of punctuation, grammar and spelling.

A. Grammarly

This tool can help you identify and correct mistakes. It can also suggest alternatives to express your thoughts. It assists you in fixing punctuation, spelling, and grammar problems. It also helps you edit sentence that is grammatically accurate, but unclear or ambiguous.

When you go through your text with Grammarly so that you're get rid of mistakes to a great extent. The software is accessible for smartphone and computer users.

B. Hemingway: this tool assists in correcting grammar errors and complicated sentences. It accomplishes this through highlighting the sentences to be corrected by using various shades, with each being a different significance.

C. Microsoft word.

It is among the most well-known platforms for typing, as well as all the required editing. Beyond the direct typing on your media platform you can make use of these tools to gain the most diverse options that can be explored using. It is likely that you won't actually do much with the latter.

Microsoft Word is available both in the computer and mobile versions.

D. Ilys

This tool lets you set your desired word count prior to you begin typing. It only permits users to modify the final word that you typed. You aren't able to edit your text until you've finished typing. However it offers a unique experience while writing.

E. The writer from the Carmly.

Despite the fact that Microsoft documents appear to be among the most widely-used tools for typing, using a carmly write helps you concentrate more on writing and how?

Once you type with it, the distracting options go away from the user interface. Additionally, it comes with "focus mode" that highlights the paragraph that you're writing.

The tools mentioned above to edit and write are available for both computers and smartphones.

2. Tool for generating ideas.

The headline for your content can be created and refined using tools such as Portent's idea generation for content Ideaflip, HubSpot's topic generator for blogs. Utilizing these tools will ensure that you have a compelling headline. It is vital to know that the most efficient ways to capture the attention of your readers and increase involvement, convert and make it SEO-friendly is by having an engaging and relevant headline.

A majority of these tools offer free versions. They are easy to use. Browse the site, type in your concept into the search engine and let it to provide you with a variety of headlines. They are easy to comprehend and use.

2. Tools for checking plagiarism

Plagiarism is a serious offense in writing, specifically in the academic and business cycle. Websites can be flagged as plagiarism-related. In reality the opposite is true. No client would wish to trust an author who's work contains plagiarism, which can lead to loss for the writer on his end. In addition, in addition to being a criminal offense as well as an attack on your integrity and could ruin your writing career in the future.

Website that examines plagiarism

* Copyscape.com
* Grammarly.com
* Writecheck.com
* Plagscan.com
* Turnitin.com
* Plagium.com
* Scanmyessay (paid offline tool)

* Plagiarism-detect.com
* Smallseotools.com/plagiarism-checker
Certain of these websites are free, while some are paid. Check them out and begin using. Be sure to subject your writing to plagiarism checks prior to publishing.

4. Word Counter

Professional writers understand the significance of using a word counters. Writing jobs typically have a specific word count. You need to adhere to it. Additionally it is recommended to write shorter than the maximal word count particularly when writing content intended for competition.

The application is available on IOS and Google Play Store on mobile devices and can also be downloaded on computers.

5. Multimedia for making visual

There are tools to assist you in increasing participation on social media as well as other platforms. This will help you gain influence and reach a larger audience. These tools can be used to make videos such as infographics, memes and infographics. images using canva, crello snappa, vennagage, snappa infographic video maker , and more. You're provided with the tools you need. The applications are on the internet for download.

6. Tools to help plan the creation of content

It is crucial to have a an organizer that is digital, to-do lists calendars, calendars, workflow planning as well as file sharing for you to finish the editing process in time and on time. To make sure you meet deadlines tools such as hotsuit tremolo, woven, wunderlist and more are crucial and can be found in the apps stores.

As a writer in the 21st century and knowing that millions of articles are published every minute, the necessity for these tools cannot be understated. They are extremely helpful for planning and creating organized calendars that can reduce distractionsto a great extent.

Chapter 14: Search Experience

This chapter isn't what you'll read in every other book that focuses on writing. Sorry for the lack of quotes from motivational speakers, but this book is focused on making you smarter, more effective and more efficient at writing.

If you're a voracious reader, then you've probably come across some written work particularly research-related work in which you were amazed by certain of the facts presented and wondered how the author/writer could have gotten these facts.

The majority of people do not know about this. Many people think of Google as the sole search engine on the planet that leaves them with the option of beckoning on it each whenever they have to look up information on the Internet. It's worth noting that, even though Google is considered to be the best search engine, it's far from being the sole search engine available in the world. In reality, Yandex is the most searched-for searching engine within Russia as well as, Baidu searches are extremely well-known in China.

For a greater knowledge base and expertise as an author it is essential to use various search engines. This will put you on the path to distinctiveness and a profound outcome.

The top 12 best search engines around the globe

* Google.com
* Bing.com
* Yahoo.co.uk
* Baidu.com
* Aol.com
* Ask.com
* Excite.com
* Duckduckgo.com
* Wolframalpha.com
* Yandex.com
* Lycos.com
* Chacha.com

Bing, Yandex and Yahoo are also very popular.

Below is the same query that has two search results

A lot of people are unaware of the way search engines function and the advantages of being able to study the same topic through multiple channels. It's a very effective tool for an experienced researcher or writer. Search results that might not be precise and clear within a search engine might be clearer and more exact in another.

Chapter 15: Rewriting Skills

Since the invention online, the the markets for information around the globe is now a global. In actual fact, re-using information is an essential aspect of the present world as millions of pieces of content are posted through the Internet each day. Many are not even delivered to their intended audience because of the an unsuitable platform or site inadequate advertising or lack of imagination of the author. In reality, you only have 30 seconds to impress your viewers due because there's a huge variety of content available on the internet , and distractions are almost inevitable. People tend to skim and reading only when they're captivated or when your content offers something of value that addresses their current needs, such as how to grow their businesses and earn more money, how to stay healthy, and so on.

Rewriting skills are crucial in helping you create quicker and more effective content to keep up with deadlines. If you possess the ability to convey your ideas in simple and more precise terms, coupled with a solid research background Your content is guaranteed to be distinctive, unique and may even garner more attention than the original writer or author.

What are the implications of rewriting

Simply put, it's the ability to create or sketch something similar with different words and layout to give better results , without having to copy someone who has done it before.

List of websites where you can get content for re-writing

Here are some websites where you can obtain an article written in the most diverse ways.

* Www.ezinarticle.com On that website, the articles are well organized all you have to do is click on the category of your article and choose the category you want to choose. For every category you choose, there's a sub-category for you to select according to your requirements.The content is well-organized on the majority of these websites but there are some

variations to a few which require you to find your preferred subject , with the appropriate topic. You can also sign up on these sites and write articles to increase your authority on the internet engines as a writer.

Use Google Translator to assist with RE-WRITING

Most people are unaware of the fact Google offers a variety of ways to move from one language to the next through its translator. Google operates in a way so that content specific to a specific geographical or language isn't readily accessible to other languages or geographic area. For instance, a lot of documents created and released in Spanish is not accessible quickly by English countries, but using a translators, it's likely. Writers have to be aware of how to use Google translator for content creation.

A Spanish related article could have precisely the information your English audience would like. The content is likely to be original and free of plagiarism because they have not been written or used in that location using an alternative language. If a skilled writer has access to this content, he may modify them to suit the needs of his readers.

STEP IN USING GOOGLE TRANSLATOR TO GET CONTENT FOR REWRITING

In your browser, enter google.com and then click search.

* Enter Google translator and then click search. It will open the new Google search platform that has two different platforms to search on.

Change the language setting on the second platform for typing to the language you prefer that is different from the language you are currently using in your place of residence.

Enter your preferred search topic on the platform according to the current language. If your search topic is easy to understand and simple enough that it can be translated into another platform that you choose another language, or the one you want to.

Copy the topic and place it in Google search box and then browse through.

* The information that pops up will be displayed in the language you wish to obtain information from.

* Choose any websites that you like and click to open it.

* On the majority of websites, Google offers the option to translate the site back to your preferred language. click it to translate it back or take the content, copy it and then put in a translation software to convert it back to your preferred language.

* Once you have successfully translated it back to the default language, copy and paste it into your editing or typing tools. Read through and revise, then look for plagiarism.

Chapter 16: Spinning skill

Spinning is similar to writing. Spinning is mostly an automated rewriting process which is done with software or applications. This software generates the appearance of brand new content from existing.

It works by replacing specific phrases, words or sentences or whole paragraphs with a variety of different versions, providing an atypical variation each time. This is called Rogeting.

However, simple automated writing, also referred to as spinning, does not discern grammar or context when it comes to the use of phrases and words.

A skilled writer is able to utilize spinning to find different ways to say the same thing. However, paying close attention to ensure the message or information being passed to readers isn't lost or changed. Therefore, it is recommended to combine spinning with the use of manual writing to edit phrases or words, being off-topic.

In certain instances, people employ article spinning to produce massive content in order to fool algorithms by repeating the same information in different ways. Article spinning is a helpful tool to help writers present every sentence in a more effective version and connect similar content to different audiences.

Here's an inventory of spin tools.

1. This is a free spinning tool that lets creates unique and 100 100% plagiarism-free content.

2. This is among the most well-known FREE spinners designed for webmasters, bloggers and content writers.

The results are trustworthy and the outputs produced by this tool are totally

Unique and easy to read. Recently, 700,000 synonyms were added to the software to increase the quality of the content.

The tool is free. You can input your content at any time and it will produce the desired variations of content.

3. The software can spin 10,000 characters on its FREE version. Its paid version lets

you to rephrase your content with any trouble.

4. It is available in desktop and free web versions. Its web version can be used alongside Android, iPad and MacBook. It also has advanced features like the correction of grammar mistakes.

It comes with a free version that is best for those who are just starting out and it also comes with the option of paying for it.

5. Artificial Intelligence and natural language processing to comprehend the text and spin the content to create a new version.

Content created, are typically completely plagiarism-free and can be used in almost every language.

The article offers two plans that are paid and both come with 14 days trial version.

6. This allows artificial intelligence to comprehend and write content. Content created is unique. Wordai spinner comprehends the concept of an article and does not pick synonyms with no connection to the topic. It can be used in multiple languages.

The spinner provides a 3-day free version. Its subscription is offered on a monthly or annually.

7. This spinner is among the most advanced, making an use of Artificial Intelligence, and it can rewrite content in one click. It is compatible with 14 languages, including English. With the best spinner, you are able to add pun-related content to your blog on Word Press and the content created is completely plagiarism-free

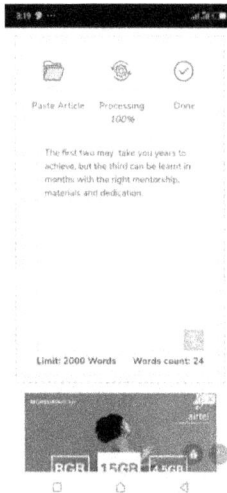

It provides three premium plans that come with a free trial . It also gives customers a 30 day money-back assurance.

8. Cleverspinner makes use of advanced artificial intelligence to select the appropriate words and synonyms. The content generated is usually understandable and original. It offers a three-day trial for free and a paid subscription afterward.

9. Spinrewriter is among the best spinners that utilizes ENL technology, which allows you to write distinctive content that is not just unique, but also has a high rank in search engines. It is the only one that offers a paid plan.

How do you use a spinning tool?

Step 1

Start your browser and type the spin website. Then click search https://smallseotools.com/article-rewriter/

Step 2

Cut and copy the information you wish to modify into the first platform for typing accessible via the web site.

Step 3.

Scroll sideways or down and click on rewrite, spin or rewrite.

Step 4

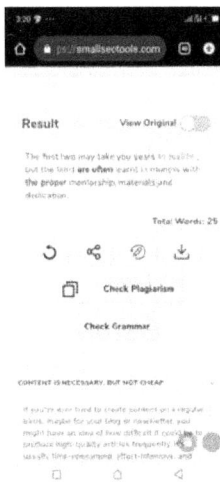

Then wait till it is loaded. Afterwards go to the second platform for the newly written content.

Chapter 17: Communities And Daily Routine

In the past couple of months, I've been able to witness what a good social network has brought to enhance my writing experience. All writers who are smart belong to successful social communities with proper consideration of the time we are in today, one in which networks can amplify the voice of the value.

The Right Community can make You a better writer

* A good social network online can help you to learn and avoid making mistakes that other writers have made at the beginning of their writing career by sharing comments and stories.

It aids you in learning new words, a new style of writing, and also helps you improve your writing skills by creating captivating written content. Are you part of an online community, and certain writers write content, they has a huge reader engagement when compared with other writers? A savvy writer will research writing by writers who have high engagement , and attempt to figure out why and how their posts are extremely popular.

Right community keeps you on the edge to learn more about and become better at your field. Nothing challenges you more than when you observe other people who are more successful that you are in your area of endeavour.

A well-established community will help to build your authority. When you publish quality content that is engaging, people will be compelled to connect with you. If you have more power, then can exert, the better chance of becoming more proficient in your writing since the drive to produce regularly more engaging content is of great importance to you.

It can help reduce the amount of redundant work, but how do you even achieve that? It is helpful to link your online social activities to writing, so that you're having fun while learning at the same time.

* You may also write a an article or story and get comments from fellow writers within this community. This lets you to gain access to punctuation, grammar, and expression.

A List of Online Communities Every Writer or Author who plans to travel the world should belong

Visit the web pages of any of the communities below to join, get involved and learn more. Don't forget the old statement that nobody is an island, not even in the realm of knowledge so, in order to develop more quickly, you must surround your self with a group of writers. These communities can comprise:

* Absolute Writer water cooler

* Critique circle

* Support group for writers who are insecure

* Next big writers

* Reddit
* Camp NaNoWriMo
* Chronicles
* Writers who help writers
* AgentQuery Connect

* Facebook groups include: The Street Team, 10 Minute Novelists, Writers Unite!, Calls for Submissions and Fiction Writers Global.

In joining an online communities such as those mentioned above it's best to look at the communities that meet your needs.

Chapter 18: Creative Writing Basics

Writing is the reverse of reading. Similar to how a child learns to listen before beginning to speak writing is a craft that requires perseverance, endurance and patience. If you're ever hoping to become the best writer you want to be it is essential to read, and read more. I don't mean to scare you. I'm aware that many are averse to reading. It's easier to sit in your sofa with your smart phone or tablet and have a chat for the entire day isn't it? Technology is in our midst, but old-fashioned methods are still effective when we are looking to expand our skills. Actually, if we mix some of the traditional concepts with the latest technologies, we'll likely to reach our goals faster and you can still keep with using your Smartphone and Tablet.

It's not necessary to take a drive or walk to the nearest bookshop to get access to reading materials. There are a lot of websites online that present interesting and insightful reading materials. Your problem might be the fact that you believe that read is dull. However, the reality is that your primary teacher might have failed to introduce you to interesting reading materials that can make you want to continue reading.

But, it's never to late. There's so much hidden in books that you'll be amazed once you have an interest. There exist books, as well as artistic pieces that can keep you at the edge of the seat for hours and you'll never be able to be able to get enough of the story. Can you be the kind of writer that keep readers engaged without not noticing the speed at which time passes? The answer is an easy yes.

Writing allows the expression of emotion and thought. Writing is an art and a skill that can be developed by using proven methods. That's right, I said "established methods'. There are research-based and tested information on how to create great creative writing materials.

Creative writing is among the numerous kinds of writing that combine entertainment and utility. It is not just a way to tell readers what to do. It isn't a sloppy guideline to solve the issue. Creative writing takes a variety of approaches to dealing the challenges of life. It is primarily used for three reasons that is:

*To instruct

*To entertain

*To stir your conscience

There are a variety of genres of writing, including short stories novels, essay writing poetry, and many other. When you begin or continue on your creative writing, you should decide on a certain subject and create the appropriate writing routine for you to become with a successful. How do you establish a consistent practice of writing to achieve the success you desire? The answer is straightforward; utilize writing prompts and exercises to gain an initial start in your writing routine. If you take on a variety of exercise and writing tasks within your writing routine and you'll end up with a draft that you can use for your writing project, be it a non-fiction creative text or a fiction piece, or poetry.

However, these writing prompts aren't going to transform your creative abilities In fact it is important to recognize that there are instances that these prompts (writing exercise and writing prompts) could lead you to a dead-end. The solution to this is to follow the prompts and write what you think of. Since the writing of different kinds of content are distinct, we will offer separate writing prompts as well as exercises for creative poetry, fiction, and non-fiction. Before we can move onto the exercises and prompts, we'll start by the the basics of writing creatively. Let's jump right into it. ....

How to Start Writing With ease

Incredibly, one of the most difficult things of writing creatively is the beginning. Many writers struggle to locate their way and get pen to paper which is often referred to as writer's block. You don't know what you want to write at this point, your mind is completely blank, leaving you in the middle of nowhere.

If you've had this happen to you don't fret because there's an escape route. How do you overcome writer's block? Here's howto:

#Brainstorm

One way to get rid of writers block can be to think. Create anything you would like to write in a random manner. Pause and go for a walk on the street or to a place that is convenient. Take the opportunity to discuss your thoughts you wrote down with someone else, and then discover the opinions of those who are in agreement with the topic you'd like to write about. Gradually, a idea of what you'd like to write about will begin to emerge in your head. The process of brainstorming can also be a time to think about what ideas you can include in the story from the numerous choices you've made. Also, you should consider where you should begin your story, and what ideas to begin with.

#Identify Your Theme

If you're looking to write a story that flows it is important to determine the message you want to communicate to the audience. Making the idea of what you truly would like to convey is essential.

Finding a subject can be the result of brainstorming.

Choose your characters

If you've got an understanding of the theme that is central to the story you want to tell It is now the right time to choose the best agents to help bring your story to completion. They are known as characters in the literary sense. It is important to create the primary character around whom the story is based. It is also important to create additional characters to fill a secondary role. The characters supporting the main character help to build an overall character. The principal character is the one who tells your story from beginning until the end. If you've read books or watched movies The end of the protagonist signifies that the story is over.

#Develop your characters

To create characters, it is important to build your characters. Find as much information regarding the character you wish to make use of as. You might think about:

Their job
-Age
-Tribe
Marital status
-Children
-Religion
-Temperament
Foods you love
-Speech
-Pets
-Appearance
Favorite sport
-Phobias
-Faults
What they love
What they hate
-Hobbies
Sleep patterns
-Occupation
-Illnesses
The Character Traits of a Few Characters and their significance to the Reader
Appearance An accurate description of what a person looks can help readers to visualize the character's image in their minds.

Action

The actions the character takes in order to aid the reader in understanding about the kind of person they are.

Speech: When a character walks and fumbles around the scene and speaks, they say. The speech can make the reader feel more connected to them as people.

It's also a good method to study the abstract features of the character by writing. It is possible to explore the characters thoughts, emotions as well as their hopes and fears through the character's thoughts and sharing it with the reader. If , for example, I'm looking to create the character of a hard-core relative in the family, it is possible to create something similar to the character, who is lean and fair skinned. She is also tall. She walks with her torso raised and is quiet in her speech. She's shy at first however, she is a ferocious inside. Amanda has a tendency to spend the majority of her time thinking of ways to disarm her twin sister, who appears to get more attention. She is a coffee lover after a morning walk around on the street with her dog. Amanda experienced an exaggerated anxiety about birds. She was screaming loudly when she saw her neighbours"duck".

A few hours later she was discovered dead, hanging from an orchard tree.

Devise conflict

Every good story is focused on a conflict of a kind. The idea should be to design the conflict into where your protagonists are to be absorbed. The conflict must mirror real-life situations that trigger distress and panic. The conflict needs to be closely connected to the main subject matter of your tale. You shouldn't create an issue that renders your characters ineffective because of their very nature they are not able to be able to effectively portray the conflict. If you're planning to discuss malice in society, that means you've chosen characters who can expose the that there is a problem. It is impossible to be a successful athlete, an honest pastor as well as an honest judge innocent children.

When you are developing an ongoing conflict, you must attempt to have your protagonist make decisions that can cause them to be in trouble. The choices must have results that create a problem for the protagonist. The reader must be shocked by the choices that the protagonist chooses to make. The reader should then discover the consequences of such difficult choices. These kinds of experiences and choices are best seen by the reader when they are based on the real world. It could be a loss of someone dear to you, playing or even a recuperation from a chronic disease.

Make the Climax

You must think of the most fascinating aspect of your story before beginning writing. Choose what that part is. It should be the pivotal the story. In an climax, your reader's emotions are pushed to the edge. There should be enough tension, tension and fear close to the final scene.

A climax can be usually about an unexpected surprise an unexpected revelation or a shocking twist.

Choose Your Point of View

The story can be told using three different perspectives. Each one of them offers the writer with a variety of options the writer. Certain viewpoints are preferred over others based on the kind of writing you do. You can generally decide to tell a story from

The 1st person perspective

* 2nd person point of view

* Third person perspective

1st Person

The first person viewpoint is one where the writer is involved with the unfolding events of the story. The most common way to describe it is using the first person pronoun , 'I'. The 1st person pronoun allows writers to convey their thoughts to the reader and to influence people to view things in a particular manner. First person narration is helpful for writing essays that are imaginative and reflect the personal experiences of real everyday life experiences. It is a disadvantage because it involves blocking out the possibility of writing fiction. It's impossible to penetrate the characters' minds and articulate what they are thinking. Also, it limits the narrator to one place at the same time. It's largely based on the words of the writer and thinks.

2nd person

The reader is a participant as a participant in the narrative. The reader is an actor. It is a character who uses the pronoun 2nd person, 'you". The reader is addressed directly, and becomes a subject throughout the narrative. It tends to explore a variety of matters that are more affecting readers more than other people. It is generally aimed at investigating the mind of the reader, and presents various possibilities. It encourages the reader to think about themselves and evaluate the value about their behavior. It's conversational, and pretty casual.

3rd person

It is, in fact, an extremely commonly used perspectives that is used in all kinds of writing. Certain kinds of writing like academic writing require third person narrative since it is thought to be objective. This is also used in fiction writing, as well as numerous other genres that require imagination. The third person employs the pronouns 'it','she' and 'he''. The writer is able to enjoy the privilege of being present in many locations at once. The third person narrator can be called the all-encompassing narrator. You have the chance to convey your characters' thoughts and feel. You can even speculate on the potential outcomes of your character's actions. You can move locations within a fraction of a second and write about events that are in a different location simultaneously as you describe other events happening in other places. The writer is not in the event. It's an impartial description of happenings in the moment you observe them. Also, it has the element of realism as the author does things that are impossible to do, such as being able to discern what the characters think.

Use the Dialogue to help you.

Dialogue is one of the techniques employed by writers to highlight the distinctive human traits characters have. It is the dialogue between two or more persons. It is an ideal way to capture human tensions, anxieties and fears. In the subsequent dialogue the reader is able to observe and watches the characters react to events in a humane manner. The actions are intended to provide the reader with what's on their minds. The reader should be able to see character lean forward as they listen to what the other characters speak, look at certain words, fold their hands or smile when they hear good news, or cross their hands and so on. When a dialogue is well-crafted each participant gets an opportunity to share their own story. They are allotted time and space in various paragraphs. As dialogue unfolds the writer will make remarks about the events unfolding. It is usually in parenthesis or in speech tags based on the style of writing.

Also, you should be able to describe the actions of the speaker. Do not leave any statements unfinished, regardless of the dialogue that they are involved in; "Where is my laptop?", asked Kenzy with a worried expression. "It's gone," said Demba turning away from Kenzy's gaze. Speech tags are used to describe the character's situation and feelings. It is not sufficient to quote speeches without explaining the context and reactions to these events of the protagonists. The explanations provide the reader with a better their understanding of the unfolding events.

Context and Setting

Nothing enhances your writing as the right setting. Setting refers to the physical setting that the events are taking place when you write. It also refers to the environment within which the events occur. The characters in your story must be in the same physical place within the reader's mind. It is also important to provide specifics of the scene. Remember you must only provide specific details that are relevant to the plot. Your character should be in a specific location such as a bed in a hospital and describe the surroundings. It is possible to mention the existence of the other hospital patients. It is important to note that providing information like 'the doctor walked into the drawer, grabbed the bottle of painkillers, gave it to the nurse , and gave her the responsibility of administering medication to the patient' a flims description. The main point is that the patient was provided painkillers. The pull of the cabinet is not a significant addition to the the story.

Beyond simply selecting a location and the description of a setting the writing can gain shine when you draw the attention of the senses. Make use of expressive adjectives in order to convey the setting in which you tell the tale. You can also include the sun as well as winter, dark, wind, rain hills, river, and the sun in an in-depth descriptions. Engaging the senses in writing can help readers to imagine the place and feel connected to the characters. If you're writing about an individual who was caught in freezing conditions, you can write "She tried to keep warm and tried to make an open fire under a tree. It was possible to see clouds of vapor escape from her mouth, she shivered, she screamed and gathered herself. Her teeth gnashed. There were goose pimples visible appearing all over her naked skin from an in-between distance. She coughed, sneezed and coughed repeatedly. ..."

A description like this can help the reader connect to cold weather and sympathize with the person in question. The reader is able to experience the feeling and is able to feel the same as the character.

The Plot

An outline is the sequence of elements of the course of a story. A good writer should plan the flow of events that occur in your story. It is important to know in advance the sequence of events and when it will happen. Set the events up so that they end in a dramatic unfolding. The events you choose to include should reflect the main themes in the narrative and evoke emotions.

The Climax

The conclusion is the most important point of an epic story. A well-written story should include action and emotions until the emotion needs to be squelched. The story ends with dramatic ways. It is at this point that the unexpected occurs and things change to the worse or better. It could be due to a decision that is contrary to the norm or recognition of something that has been hidden and alters the lives for the protagonist, specifically the protagonist or the solution to an issue that has caused trouble, pain and pain for a long time.

The End of Your Story

The best story ever written is not without a conclusion. The ending is what makes or break a work of art. A satisfying ending usually provides the reader with a solution in some way. There are some resolutions that may not be obvious. But, the narrative must demonstrate some sort of change. It is possible to present this ending in the form of:

Characters that show a different view of the world. They might also display a type of transformation.

Open ending "She turned her head and laughed. He then turned around and went away from the stage."

Resolved: Maria watched in awe as Shikumba loaded his belongings into the car before driving off.

Similar to the beginning: He walked into the room wearing a yellow suit, an unusual shade for man's attire.

*Monologue: These are comments from characters, "if only I had told my father that I was planning to go to on the beaches ...."'

Image: "Now the birds could sing to the trees one again. The sound of the mills for cereal could be heard once more. The life recommenced in the barren plains."

The symbolism is: "I saw the crow fly through the sky at the horizon. the clouds changed from grey to orange and then red. The owl sat on the cedar tree nearby."

Note

The choice of location will have some value. If you choose to place your story in the desert, the circumstances can help in making the story compelling. The desert's environment should serve as the catalyst for certain circumstances that wouldn't occur in a different environment. The setting must be in sync with the plot.

Once you've mastered the basics of writing, we'll take a look at what you've learned through the writing questions and exercises. Apply the most you've learned regardless of whether you're writing nonfiction, fiction, or poetry.

Chapter 19: Creativity Prompts, Along With Exercises For Non-Fiction

These writing exercises that are listed in this guide will assist you to become creative and write in the context of everyday things and routines.

Popular holiday/event

Select a fas-filled celebration in your nation or around the globe and concentrate on the elements that make the event unique. The event could involve Christmas, Idd the holidays, thanksgiving, or new year. The most memorable part of the occasion for you. It could be the recipe creating that special meal. Define what makes it unique.

Fate

If you take a look back at your life, choose one event from your life that occurred through random chance or a single decision that transformed your life in some way. The event could have been an accident encounter with a stranger that transformed your life or even helped you look at your life in a different way. It could also be an accident that you took the wrong bus and were stranded in the middle of nowhere and was able to meet your soulmate. Because we all is likely to have many of these experiences, you can combine them all into one.

Define the reason for the event

This could mean Valentine's Day, New Year's Eve, or any other celebration. Explore the myths and the facts of the celebration If you choose Boxing day, explain what the intention behind the gifts and the magi who is generous.

Shock messages

It's usually hard to send messages that are difficult to understand. It's even more difficult receiving these messages. Consider an enthralling message you'd wish to share with someone. What would be your ideal method of communication? Do you prefer to call or message a person. What effect would it have when you asked a complete stranger to convey the message? If you used a non-conventional method such as graffiti in the bathroom to deliver your message!

Heights

Imagine the most difficult climb you've ever attempted. Note down the way the climb was. It could be a mountain or a tall structure. Imagine how you felt as you looked down upon having reached the top. Would you do the same hike? If you had the chance to climb the famous mountain of fame, tell us how you was like after completing your ideal climb. Are you the same famed as you hoped? What experiences would you want to impart to novices who are in the same situation? What amazing events did youor someone you traveled with, encounter? If you were part of a group what was the benefit of having others with you on the mountain? What would you have done by yourself? What myths do you want to debunk? What's your next ploy?

A letter addressed to you

Take a look at how you live your day and what happens that surround it. Consider those things that make you feel disappointed and the things that inspire your heart, and the ones that make you smile and worry about. Write down the things you'd rather hear others speak to you about. Review your own self, and then praise and criticize your character. Enjoy yourself by sharing insights into your life. Consider things that concern or trouble you, and also those that hinder you from reaching your goals. It is possible to recall an event that you regret or even celebrate. If it's an action which you regret, think that you were the person that the incident directly affected and tell yourself what they would have written to you, or what they would have shared with you in an honest evaluation of the incident. Inflate your self-esteem to tell yourself some amazing things. Write a positive, honest letter to yourself, as if it was written by a trustworthy friend.

Classic songs that you love

Tell us about a song that you loved when you were young, maybe when you were in the teen years. Tell us how you felt about the music and how you feel about it today. Be specific about any changes in your tastes or your interest in particular music genres. Describe the songs you are listening to as you age. Speak about when they sound better.

Halloween Costumes

Tell us about your favorite and most terrifying Halloween costume. Explain why it scares your the most. Describe the costume in detail and tell us what makes it the most terrifying for you.

A person of inspiration or the muse

Tell us why this muse has been an inspiration to you. Write about the moments in the life of the person who cause you to want to live your life and be the best at the things you do. Concentrate on the unique and distinctive characteristics of this unique person.

Surprised by a New Discovery

Tell us about an event in which you came across an object or a person who led you to discover something important within your own life. Discuss the excitement of the discovery , and the effect it had on you or someone else.

Poetry Prompts

Poetry is an unplanned part of writing. These writing concepts for creative writing will stimulate your creativity and broaden your understanding of poetry.

Anonymous Thanks

Poems about the concept of thanksgiving is among your options for prompts, particularly when it's close or during the time of Giving. Select someone you'd like to acknowledge and write about the way they inspire you to acknowledge them and the things you value about them. It could be your mother, father or a friend. However this could also be an overall message of thanks to people all over the world. It could also be addressed towards The Supreme Being.

Words on the street

You can also write a piece about an issue you'd like the world to be aware of. Imagine if you had the opportunity to write about your thoughts in big bold letters that were hung on one of the sides of your most tall buildings or on billboards in front of everyone to view.

Your shadow

Consider your shadow. What are the characteristics that amaze you in your shadow? Imagine that you get up in the morning only to discover that your shadow has gone. Consider the shadow of your loyal companion who will never leave you. Imagine what your shadow does or appears in the dark. Is it aware that you are there? Think about the "what you're doing" and the "what isn't."

Death

Death is a great source of poetry material. Find out the origins of death. How do you interpret the symbolism meanings of death? Imagine if death was not a reality to the world; how would the world look like?

The house was haunted and taunted by ghosts

Haunted houses are a fascinating source of stories across the globe. This is an excellent option to talk about the macabre and the ghostly. Discuss the strange creaks, and the mysterious fire incidents in the haunted home you resided in. Discuss the sounds that echoed off the roof, the dark corridors , and those creaking floors.

Traumatic Event

Think of an incident which caused you pain or loved ones. Define the cause. The cause could include war, or even an accident. This could involve a boat that was sunk, or a train wreck. Explain how it happened and what happened. The feeling of helplessness felt by the victims.

Catastrophe

Tell us about a natural disaster that you experienced or encountered. The event could have been a tornado or tsunami, lightning strike, or hurricane. Define the emotion you experienced when you are in the midst of a catastrophe. Explore the feeling of helplessness for humanity in such disasters. What was the significance of the incident to you?

Ode

Feel the frustration of not having something you'd like to have. Consider the implications that you do not have it. What would happen if you did? What would your daily life be like? You can also write about your deep-seated feelings towards the person or thing you love.

A fear

Discuss your most feared fears. Examine the fear and write about the absurdity. Consider the causes of these fears.

Sound

Imagine the sounds you hear in your daily life. You should try to look beyond the sound on the wall. It could be the sounds that people are making around you in the office, on the bus or at the market. Discuss them and what they will be that you wouldn't hear them any more.

Anaphora

Write poems that begin with the similar phrases or words. The similarities create an interesting rhythm.

The window

Consider the time you look out the window of your office or home. Imagine what you can observe. Think about what you can observe when you look out the window. It might be stormy, snowstorm, a blizzard, flowers and so on. Imagine what it would look like if the window weren't there. If your roommates are looking through the same window are they seeing similar things? Discuss the peace and safety that the room offers.

Family Focus

Each family is unique and has their own own antics, personalities, highs and lows. Name the people in your family and the most memorable moments and the black sheep that you perceive to be The greedy, the insecure, the supportive and the most popular, and all.

Exercises, Prompts and Ideas for Fiction

Writing fiction can be fun, but it requires you to be on your element. By using these writing prompts it shouldn't be difficulty creating your own creative flow.

I am stuck in an Elevator

The feeling of being stuck in an elevator is a frightening experience for everyone; it's one of those experiences that make you shiver to the core. It's a fantastic event to inspire your fiction writing since the reader experiences the terror along with the victims. Discuss what you are talking about in those moments of tension.

The cat

You can begin your story with a cat. Cats are often associated with mystery, and ghosts too. They can be used to create mysterious events that can be linked to the personality of a cat.

From the Corner of Your Eye

Begin your story by... It was like I noticed some sort of flash in the air. It was a quick glance out of my vision. I didn't notice it until I looked back. I was thinking it was an illusion. Alas! I was mistaken...

Imagine that you were a Ghost

Write about events from the viewpoint of ghosts. Imagine what you believe to be the character of a ghost, and then relate your story from that perspective. It's an interesting perspective that will definitely provide an exciting new reading.

Change in Gender Roles

Imagine a scenario in which the role of gender in the society are suddenly changed. Consider the new challenges. You can create an individual who is trying to figure out how to live the new world.

The Beast's Name In You

Consider the animal part that is within you. Tell the story that draws you into the role of an animal.

Long Flight to the Future

Consider the world in the next ten years. Do you have a description of what the world will be? Consider the technologies of today. Imagine how certain aspects today might look in retrospect. Imagine what your future with your friends are now. Consider the essentials of daily life. Find out the options for transportation , and then. Do you think there would be a lot of tourists. Imagine a world in which you're part of the tourist spots in the next ten years.

Children Seated on a Log next to a River

Imagine what children would be talking about to one another. Make a sudden turn in which the children are in danger.

Ominous Asteroid

Discuss an ominous asteroid that was heading towards earth. Recall the sensation as the entire town stood in amazement, swarmed and attempted to flee from the impending disaster.

A Bench with a Friend in the Park

Write about a gentle man who was sitting on an outdoor bench on a snowy cold day. Explain how you came to realize that his innocent look was the perfect disguise for a murderous criminal. Explain the sudden transformation and the person who was the victim.

A Chilling Proclamation

Imagine a doctor who is calmly and gently informs his pregnant patient, "Mom, one of you will live and however, not both... I'm sorry".

If you've been practicing creative writing prompts and ideas The next step is learning some useful techniques and tricks to help you become more creative and write.

Writing away from the table

What you need to be aware of as a aspiring writers is that all writing usually begins by generating some kind of inspiration. This inspiration is stimulated by a myriad of experiences, people or ideas. Thus, writing starts in your head before you translate it into the paper. This is why it's crucial to remain aware that any place you visit or stop can be a source for writing. What should you do?

You can keep a diary or Notebook

The practice of keeping a journal or notebook is beneficial to new writers. Even experienced writers will note important events from their lives wherever they travel. Writing, especially creative writing, is an expression of the reality of our lives.

It is a good habit to note the thoughts that pop into your head. It happens everywhere: at night, in the plane, bus or even at the table. The possibilities are endless. There's no way to predict what unique and intriguing idea will pop up in your head. Take your notebook everywhere you go and note down any quotes you encounter, intriguing comments questions, experiences, and much more.

Write a few lines Everyday

Create a habit of writing even if you're not feeling like doing it. Be aware that habits develop. You'll soon be able to write without prompts from your own or from an external sources.

Collect Stories

People are a fascinating source of information that you can incorporate into your story. Take note of the stories you share with your friends everywhere you travel. Keep track of the odd and the wacky or the shocking interesting and make use of them to improve your writing. Of course, you can't utilize all of them. But, you've got an abundance of sources to seek to and choose interesting parts from in order to make your writing compelling.

Read More, Read, Continue to Read Some More

The exposure to various forms of writing can help you create an individual style by combining the lessons you've learned from others. Don't limit yourself to one type of writing. However, it's an ideal idea to begin with the things that interest you the most and to develop an practice of reading.

As you record moments that you could write about You must know exactly the way that you would like it flow. This is why you need a clear outline from the very beginning. How do you arrange everything to ensure that each piece is perfectly positioned? Let's find out next.

Structure

To create an end product that is polished to sell it, you need to pack it properly. Additionally, you must make use of words in as to be in line with to what you want. Remove ambiguity by keeping an eye for misplaced prepositions as well as adjectives and Adverbs. Language usage is influenced by various prevailing conditions. It is important to think about questions like how old the person speaking as well as the age of people in the audience, and the effect of what is said on the audience and the things you plan to draw conclusions on the many conversations. It is also important to compose your work in a manner that makes it simple for readers to follow.

Divide your essay into an introduction, and then the principal body/chapters, in which the details are revealed and then provide a conclusion or the summary.

*Paragraphing: Writing needs to be written in paragraphs in order to avoid the impact of looking at a huge piece of writing that seems to be insurmountable for the person reading it. The introduction should be given an additional paragraph. This is to notify the reader to what you are planning to write. A well-written introduction should include a topical sentence in your introduction.

A topic sentence outlines the direction of the writing but it isn't definitive. For example, if you want to write an essay on euthanasia, write "Euthanasia is a topic that is controversial that conservatives have reasons to oppose it, and modern medical science appears to provide an argument that is convincing in its favor, even though there is room for more debate." The above example is a common college argumentative essay.

Conclusion

Thank you for downloading the book!

I hope that this book was capable of providing you with more suggestions in the process of improving your writing skills and improving your writing generally. You do not need to not be doing or experiencing something extraordinary in order to move things forward. In some cases, it's just the most basic of things that can inspire people the most. The only thing you have to do is do a bit of mental and physical work to discover the inspiration.

Thanks and best of luck!

www.ingramcontent.com/pod-product-compliance
Lightning Source LLC
Chambersburg PA
CBHW071218210326
41597CB00016B/1861